Bob Hope

Bob Hope

Jenny Curtis

MetroBooks

MetroBooks

An Imprint of Friedman/Fairfax Publishers

Library of Congress Cataloging-in-Publication Data

Curtis, Jenny, 1970–

Bob Hope / by Jenny Curtis.

    p.   cm.

ISBN 1-56799-854-2

Hope, Bob, 1903–   . 2. Comedians—United States—Biography.

1. Title.

PN2287.h63C87   1999

792.7'028'092—dc21

[b]   99-17310

                                                                                                         CIP

Editor: Celeste Sollod

Art Director: Jeff Batzli

Designer: Jeanne Dzienciol

Photography Editor: Jennifer Bove

Printed by Sing Cheong Printing Company Ltd. in Hong Kong

Color separations by Ocean Graphics Arts Ltd.

Printed in China by Sing Cheong Printing Company Ltd.

For bulk purchases and special sales, please contact:

Friedman/Fairfax Publishers

Attention: Sales Department

15 West 26th Street

New York, NY 10010

212/685-6610 FAX 212/685-1307

Visit our website:

http://www.metrobooks.com

For the Hegi family,
whose hospitality, support and memories made this possible.

Acknowledgments

Thanks to Celeste Sollod for all her help and encouragement.

Special thanks to Jessie, Graham, and Kakalios

for putting up with my ravings.

Contents

A MAN OF CONTRADICTIONS

Bob Hope is a man of contradictions. His persona is that of an unlikable fellow with whom we can nevertheless sympathize, because we never fully believe him to be real. People accept Bob Hope's wisecracking, cowardly character as a cartoon. It is part of his self-deprecating style that he allows himself to be seen in such an unflattering light.

In *Caught in the Draft* he was a coward afraid to shoot a gun, while in reality Hope put himself in harm's way repeatedly by entertaining the troops in four wars. Bob Hope is the multimillionaire who made his writers for the *Pepsodent Radio Hour* radio show go out and buy him ice cream every week, but left none for them. He is also one of the most generous patrons of charity the world has ever known. In countless sketches and films he's played an incorrigible yet luckless skirt chaser, when in reality he has been happily married for more than sixty years. In his three hundred television specials he was the comic dependent on writers and cue cards, but offstage he was known to his close friends as a naturally funny man with an insatiable need to hear others laugh at his jokes. To hundreds of thousands of GIs and their families he was a great American patriot, yet he is an English-born actor. He was a friend to six Democratic presidents through ten administrations. Jimmy Carter paid Hope the ultimate compliment in 1980 by joking, "I've been in office 489 days. In three weeks more I will have stayed in the White House as many times as Bob Hope has." But Hope in his personal politics is a somewhat hawkish Republican. He is a layabout who gets lucky and reclines smugly on a satin couch with Dorothy Lamour in *Road to Morocco,* but in reality he was an indefatigable showman. In his sixties he performed in Vietnam with an energy equal to that of his costars, most of whom were one-third his age. A vaudevillian in temperament, he was willing to go almost anywhere at any time as long as he had an audience.

Opposite: **Bob Hope was a star of radio and Broadway before moving to the silver screen and, later, television.** Right: **Hope entertained his studio audience at a taping of his NBC radio show around 1953. He has mixed comedy and dance since his vaudeville days, billing himself as a "dancemedian."**

Chapter 1

FROM VAUDEVILLE TO BROADWAY

Above: **Early in his career, Les Hope was part of a vaudeville duo; in the 1920s, he and Lloyd "Lefty" Durbin pieced together an act from old comedy routines and novelty dance steps.** Opposite: **Long before he made his professional debut, Leslie Hope, the future Bob Hope, had a dramatic flair and a love of the stage; here the youngster poses on a paper moon at Luna Park in Ohio.**

Bob Hope was born Leslie Townes Hope, the fifth of seven sons of William Henry "Harry" and Avis Hope, on May 29, 1903, in Eltham, England.

His father was a stonemason, his mother a concert singer. William Hope struggled to provide for his family in an era when the craft of stonemasonry was disappearing in favor of mass-produced bricks. He frequently left the family home to take work in nearby towns, and the Hopes moved often throughout Leslie's childhood, migrating from Wales to Bristol and eventually to Cleveland, Ohio, where they became naturalized citizens of the United States in 1920.

Avis and her seven sons all had to pitch in and work. The older boys abandoned school as soon as possible to help provide for the family. Avis was able to save up enough money from her job to buy a spinet, a small harpsichord, and it was at home in Cleveland that Leslie first learned to perform, singing duets to his mother's piano accompaniment. He first became involved with the world of show business when he entered a Charlie Chaplin–imitation contest at the age of nine.

In 1967, while doing a benefit for the Boys Club of Cleveland, Hope quipped about his rough-and-tumble youth, "I came from a pretty tough neighborhood. We'd have been called juvenile delinquents only our neighborhood couldn't afford a sociologist." Hope's mother and older brothers worried about Les, who had quit school as soon as he legally could, drifting from one part-time job to the next and spending too much time hanging out at pool halls. Hope's family didn't understand that his interest in performing was more than a passing fancy. He wanted to be a professional entertainer and was willing to do whatever it took to become one.

STEPPING OUT

In his spare time, Hope studied dancing and singing with local performers. In 1921, when he was eighteen, he formed his first vaudeville act with his girlfriend, Mildred Rosequist.

Hope worked odd jobs during the day—at various times he was a pool shark, an amateur boxer, and an assistant in his brother Fred's butcher shop. About his boxing career, Hope later joked, "I fought under the name Rembrandt Hope, I was on the canvas so much." Actually, Hope fought under the name Packy East, a pun on the name of the famous boxer Packy West. Hope was unable to find a day job that made him feel as good as his limited forays into show business did, so he continued to work on his act. In the evenings, he devoted himself to his true passion—the desire to become an entertainer.

Les and Mildred worked on their dance routines through the night in her mother's kitchen after her family had gone to bed. The couple would dine on meat that Leslie had pinched from his brother's shop. After he left Mildred's, often in the middle of the night, he would take a streetcar across town to meet with a vocal quartet. Despite his dogged devotion to show business, Hope never admitted to the hard work. "I decided to forget about getting a job and earning a living and stayed with show business," he later quipped. And it

Above left: **In 1891, Harry and Avis Hope were a young Welsh couple: he was a bricklayer, and she was an aspiring concert singer. Avis was fifteen when she married Harry Hope and began a family.** Above right: **Four of their seven boys—Leslie (who would later change his name to Bob), Fred, Jack, and Sid— stand on the family porch in Cleveland, Ohio.**

> **"I fought** under the name **Rembrandt** Hope, I was on **the canvas** so much.**"**
>
> —*Bob Hope*

Right: **The Great White Hope: Bob Hope poses in a promotional still for his 1952 film *Military Policeman*, but this wasn't his first trip into the ring. As a young man in Cleveland, he had a brief career as a boxer.**

Opposite: **Mildred Rosequist and Leslie Hope were partners in what was Les' first vaudeville act. The couple performed in the style of Fred and Irene Castle, the most famous dancing couple of the 1920s. Les and Mildred were also romantically involved, and when they broke up, so did the act.**

was this constant appearance of enjoying himself that audiences picked up on throughout his career. His attitude was infectious, and soon, no matter what the situation or the gag, audiences would find that they, too, were enjoying themselves.

THE JOLLY FOLLIES

In 1924, it became apparent that Mildred was more interested in marriage than show business. She and Hope separated, and he formed an act with local dance-hall ham Lefty

Vaudeville: Hollywood's Training Ground

Bob Hope wasn't the only movie star to start out in vaudeville. Among others, Cary Grant and James Cagney tried vaudeville, although they met with little success. Both Grant and Cagney were guests of the magnanimous Eddie Foy, whom Hope later played in the film *The Seven Little Foys*. The star vaudevillian was famous for inviting down-and-out bit players to his table and picking up the tab.

George Burns and Gracie Allen were two of the biggest stars of vaudeville at the time Hope was starting out. The young comedian borrowed their famous straight man, ditsy woman routine for his radio programs and movies.

Bob Hope and Bing Crosby also play vaudevillians at the start of *Road to Bali*. They even repeat a variation on an old routine that Hope used in his vaudeville act. Bing walks across the stage with a pair of nylon stockings, and Bob asks, "Where are you going?" to which Bing replies, "Out to get these filled."

Durbin, whose style he admired. The pair opened for tab shows (short musical comedies) and for a down-on-his-luck Fatty Arbuckle. Yearning to do comedy, Hope molded the act around the comic stunt segments. Upon the recommendation of Arbuckle, Les and Lefty, as they were billed, were picked up by Fred Hurley, who produced a tab show on the midwestern circuit called the Jolly Follies.

The life of nonheadlining vaudevillians could be workaday and grim. The troupes were housed in spartan boarding houses, with the sexes strictly segregated. Hope became involved in a scandal when he developed a cold and elicited sympathy from an attractive pianist, Kathleen O'Shea. She brought him back to her room to rub a home-remedy balm on his chest. In a scene that could have come from one of his movies, the pair were discovered in her room, with a shirtless Hope trying to talk his way out of the jam. He was kicked out of his own boarding house and nearly lost his job over the incident.

The Jolly Follies was small-time, but Les was learning new skills that would help him get into the big leagues. Although Lefty was thought by all in the troupe to be the real comedian, Les got a chance to show them differently in 1924 in Bloomington, Indiana. Hope was asked to fill in on one of the straight comedy segments, a skit called "Country Store Night," in which he played the emcee of a make-believe hillbilly variety hour. His lines "killed," and the emcee who would later become known to the world as Bob Hope was born.

In 1925, tragedy hit the Jolly Follies when Lefty died of tuberculosis. The cramped living conditions, poor diet, and demanding schedule had been too much for Durbin. Hope was strongly affected by his death and, at least in part, by the realization that it could have just as easily been him. Les found a new partner, George Byrne, and they quickly put together a new act called the Eccentric, which was built around a comic dance style. Hope yearned to be more than a dancer, and he and Byrne continued to pad out their act with comic skits. The two retooled old vaudeville routines and stole jokes from magazines. Hope would play straight man to Byrne, who would walk across the stage with a dress on a hanger. Hope would ask, "Where are you going?" to which Byrne would reply, "Out to get this filled." The comic pair became more popular and soon they were headlining the Follies. In 1926, when they realized that they'd outgrown the Hurley troupe, Hope and Byrne struck out on their own. With a new act called the Dancing Demons, the pair set out on the midwestern vaudeville circuit.

A COMEDIAN IS BORN

There was nothing particularly original about Byrne and Hope. Their act was pieced together out of fairly standard routines, but fresh material wasn't necessary in small-town houses. If anything, audiences preferred a familiar joke, if it was done well, to the more sophisticated

Left: **Lefty and Les in vaudeville in the 1920s. Lefty was considered the comedian and Les was the act's straight man.**
Right: **As a lithe 16-year-old newcomer to vaudeville, Leslie Hope hadn't quite grown into his profile, or his bowler hat.**

> **"** My **first day of school** in Cleveland the other kids asked me, 'What's your name?' When I said 'Les Hope,' they switched it to **Hopeless.**"
>
> —*Bob Hope*

topical humor that was becoming popular in big cities on the East Coast. The Dancemedians, as Byrne and Hope billed themselves, got a big break in 1927 when they got a part in the hit Broadway show *The Sidewalks of New York.* They were hired as specialty dancers with bit speaking parts. After a few months with *Sidewalks,* Hope and Byrne were cut from the show to make room for a bigger-name specialty dancer. They played a few more shows together on the strength of their Broadway credentials, but split up when Les made the decision to go solo.

In the first few months of 1928, Hope played shows in Cleveland doing his new solo act, a blackface Al Jolson rip-off with a bowler and cigar. One night Hope arrived at the theater too late to put on the burnt cork that was used as blackface, but the audience liked him better without it, and the theater manager told him that his face was funny enough on its own.

Hope's face might have been funny enough on its own, but his act wasn't. He moved on to Chicago, where for six months he nearly starved while he was looking for a break. About to return home to Cleveland, he ran into Charlie Cooley, an old friend from his pool-shark days. Cooley worked for a prominent Chicago entertainment agency and helped Hope get a job as the regular emcee at the Stratford Theater.

For his new job, Hope changed his first name from Leslie to Bob to avoid the childhood tags "Less Hope" and "Hopeless." It was at the Stratford that Hope perfected his gift for comic timing. He discovered that if he waited long enough for the audience to get a joke, he could occasionally turn a bombed gag around. The wait itself became part of the joke, and it put him in control of the crowd. Hope said he waited "longer than any other comedian had the guts to wait. My idea was to let them know who was running things."

Bob took a shine to Louise Troxell, one of the regular performers at the Stratford. They started dating, and Bob began doing a regular sketch with her that was loosely patterned on

From youngest to oldest (left to right), the Hope family poses at the old homestead: George, Sid, Leslie, Jack, Fred, Jim, and Ivor. Before Leslie was born, a baby girl, Emily, had died of diphtheria.

that of George Burns and Gracie Allen. Bob fed straight lines to Louise, who'd serve up one ditsy punch line after another. The formula was a success, and Hope used it repeatedly throughout his radio and television career.

The steady gig at the Stratford was comfortable, but the theater was not considered an A-list house. Ever ambitious, Hope set out to do a tour that would end in New York and gathered a small troupe of actors, including Louise, to do an act. As his paycheck grew to around $300 a week, he hired a pair of writers to feed his need for new material.

At the end of the tour, Hope played what was then his biggest show yet, at Proctor's on 86th Street before a sophisticated Manhattan audience. Bob came out to do his monologue after the movie actress Leatrice Joy, who'd recently been involved in a scandal-ridden marriage to John Gilbert. Hope immediately made eye contact with a woman in the audience and said, "Don't worry, lady, I'm not John Gilbert." The audience loved the joke, which taught him an important lesson about varying his material for different types of audiences. Manhattanites preferred the slick, topical joke to the routines that went over big in the heartland.

MAKING IT THERE

Bob Hope's transition from New York vaudeville to Broadway was the most important step he ever took. He turned the experience into a pattern of survival that he repeated throughout his career. Although he was remarkably successful, he didn't allow himself to get comfortable in one area of entertainment. Hope had his eye on Hollywood and even did an experimental television broadcast in the early 1930s. In the late 1920s, vaudeville was a dying enterprise to which the Great Depression dealt the deathblow. Film and radio were drawing audiences away from live performances, and movie screens were frequently added to vaudeville houses. Entertainers often had to compete with movies on the same bill.

In 1930, Hope was booked at a theater to follow the great World War I drama *All Quiet on the Western Front.* As could be expected, when the lights came up after the film's harrowing conclusion, in which the main character is killed, the audience was not in the mood to laugh; Hope's act bombed. He had enough clout to get booked at another theater, but a few days into that engagement he was up against the same movie. Again his act bombed. Looking back, Hope said that he should have decided to level with the audience. Had he come onstage and actually mentioned the difficulty of following up *All Quiet on the Western Front,* he might have succeeded. It took time for Hope to learn that by letting audiences in on his troubles, he could win their sympathy. With more experience, his ability to connect with audiences under almost impossible circumstances and win them over through

Opposite: **Although Hope always played his looks and suave manner for laughs, he was one of the first comics good-looking enough to be a believable romantic lead.**

Above and opposite: **Although the young comedian had a rocky start in New York, he got a break when he was cast in the Broadway musical *Roberta*, along with Ray Middleton, Lydia Roberts, and Sydney Greenstreet** (above); **and Tamara, Fay Templeton, and George Murphy** (opposite).

the sheer force of his personality became his most important survival skill, the one that enabled him to succed in so many media

Later that year, when Bob was playing the Capitol Theater in New York, he shared a bill with a crooner named Bing Crosby. Crosby and Hope had a mutual admiration for each other's abilities from the start and decided to do a joint comedy routine for the four nights they were booked together. Since neither of them could decide who should play the straight man, they developed a sparring, slightly competitive, gently insulting routine. Crosby mocked Hope's looks, while Hope made fun of Crosby's age. The chemistry between them was pure magic, but it was years before Hollywood would turn it into box-office gold. Hope and Crosby went their separate ways after the short run for some time, and performed together only occasionally when Hope appeared on Crosby's radio show to promote his vaudeville act.

DOING GOOD

Hope understood the power of promotion and publicity. He was forever dreaming up stunts to get his name in the papers. For one important gig at New York's Palace Theater, he hired men to picket the theater wearing sandwich boards that read "Bob Hope: The Comic Find of the West." Hope also knew that good works were good publicity. As the Great Depression raged, he volunteered to emcee dozens of charity events, hosting as many as five benefits in a single day. This constant exposure was important to Hope, as it helped build his name and gave him a chance to try out monologues with audiences.

As a headliner in A-list houses, Hope made a very good living as a vaudevillian. His act earned him $500 a week, much of which was left over after he paid the performers. At a time when the median weekly income was $50 and breadlines were forming for the unemployed, it was important for entertainers to give something back. But one cannot chalk up

Although it ran through the worst of the Great Depression, *Roberta* was a smash hit when many theatrical companies were going broke. One of the main reasons for its success was its opening number, "Smoke Gets in Your Eyes."

Hope's passion for charitable works to mere ambition. His intense pace and dedication to benefit work reveal his sincerity. Having grown up in poverty himself, he could hardly ignore the desperate conditions that existed in 1930s New York. Hope's mother encouraged him to do charity work, and as she was dying of cancer, his benefit work became a kind of ongoing tribute to her values.

Benefit work helped Hope develop his typical easygoing, self-deprecating style as master of ceremonies. His ability to make an audience sympathize with him usually compensated for his frequently old or mediocre material. His act got noticed, and he was hired to play the role of Huckleberry Haines in the Broadway musical *Roberta.* It was an important break for the young vaudevillian: *Roberta* was a hit show, and he had an excellent part. When *Roberta* went on the road, Bob abandoned his old act and broke off his relationship with Louise, who had become his fiancée. The couple had gone so far as to obtain a marriage license before they realized that they had drifted apart. Louise had become interested in a piano player, and Bob was too involved in his career to take much notice.

PART OF THE ACT

A short while later, in December 1933, while working on *Roberta,* Hope was introduced to a young nightclub singer named Dolores Reade. He invited her to come around and watch him perform the next day. She did, expecting to have to strain in order to spot his ski-slope nose in the chorus. She was surprised and embarrassed when she realized that he was the second lead. Dolores didn't go backstage to meet him after the show, but left it to him to track her down again. After this unsteady start, their courtship took off with intensity. They were married two months later in Erie, Pennsylvania, not far from where Bob was performing.

Following his earlier pattern, Bob quickly worked Dolores into his act when he was sent out on a series of midwestern vaudeville gigs. Dolores would begin to sing while Bob waited in the wings. Shortly after the number began, he'd stroll onstage and sit at her feet, gaping at her with loving eyes. As she continued her song, though she was obviously distracted by his presence, he'd kiss her arm, Gomez Addams style, and nibble on her ear. Dolores later said that the key to the routine was the obvious affection between the two and that it would never have worked if they hadn't been in love. Vaudeville audiences adored the routine, but Dolores had difficulty working with her new husband; his demands of perfection made her tense. She decided that her marriage was more important than the act and retired from vaudeville after only a few performances. Later, she occasionally appeared with her husband while he entertained the troops, as when she went with him to Korea and sang such standards as "White Christmas."

Opposite: **Newlyweds Bob and Dolores Reade Hope at the start of their marriage in 1934. Bob met Dolores when he heard her sing in a New York nightclub around Christmas, and they were married the following February. Describing his wedding day, Bob said, "She had me in such a thick, pink fog."**

Bob Hope and Ethel Merman in Cole Porter's musical *Red Hot and Blue*. The show also starred Jimmy Durante. Hope observed and admired Durante at work, but he wasn't above upstaging everyone at rehearsals with an ad lib or a joke. Merman said of Hope, "He would almost rather get me or the chorus girls—or anyone on stage—laughing than the audience."

Chapter 2

RADIO
STAR

Above: **In the early days, Bob Hope joined Bing Crosby on the latter's *Kraft Hour Radio Show*. Once Hope had his own show, Crosby returned the favor. Here, Crosby shows up on Hope's *Pepsodent Radio Hour* to trade smart remarks.** Opposite: **Bob Hope started doing radio performances for NBC in 1937, beginning an association that would eventually set a record for longevity in the industry.**

Bob Hope's radio career began with his appearance on the Capitol Family Hour *to promote his vaudeville act with Bing Crosby* at New York's Capitol Theater. It was Hope's keen publicity sense that first attracted him to the medium, but he soon realized that the slump in the popularity of vaudeville was due, at least in part, to the success of free entertainment provided by radio. "The more I got into it," Hope said, "the more I saw it was the hot thing."

Hope made frequent radio appearances on Rudy Vallee's radio show, sponsored by Fleischmann's yeast, to promote his acting career in Broadway plays, such as *Red Hot and Blue.* In 1937 he was hired as a regular emcee for the *Woodbury Soap Rippling Rhythm Review.* At first, the shift to radio was difficult for Hope. He had depended on a live audience's reactions for his timing. His staccato delivery of one joke after another, with the famous Hope pause during which he took in the audience and the audience took in his last joke, didn't work with just a microphone. He realized that timing was key to a good performance on the radio. Hope studied Jack Benny's wisecracking radio family and decided to spend more time developing sketches with other performers who would help fill the void left by the lack of a live audience. One of his most popular routines was a ditsy comic duet with a character named Honey Chile, first played by the remarkable sixteen-year-old Patricia Wilder. Hope set up jokes for the soft-spoken southern dame, and Honey got all the laughs. Their flirtatious manner on the air led many to believe that there was more to their chemistry than an act, but Wilder denied the connection.

Another problem Hope faced was the adaptation of his more risqué material for radio audiences. The comedian was accustomed to a certain amount of leniency, especially in New York vaudeville houses. But radio had an even tighter censorship code than the movie industry's dreaded Hayes Code. Radio was the first mass medium to enter people's homes, and it was therefore expected to be on its very best Sunday parlor behavior. After Orson Welles'

Part of Hope's self-deprecating style was to grip the microphone in self-defense when a joke bombed. Here, he looks as though he just might brandish it as a weapon, admonishing, "Back, back!" This sort of behavior would always get a bigger laugh than any one-liner in the whole monologue.

infamous "War of the Worlds" broadcast, which terrified millions with its realistic depiction of a Martian invasion, the industry was forced to censor itself or face legislation from Washington. In the movies you could imply sexuality, but in radio you were to pretend it did not exist. The censors were so strict that they once rebuked Jack Benny for having the word "virginal" appear in the stage directions of a script. It didn't matter that the word was never said on the air; the censors insisted that it not be connected even remotely with radio.

Hope managed to tone down his act. He relied on his self-disparaging humor, such as jokes about his own cowardice, and turned off the lecherous side of his persona that would soon help make him a star in Hollywood.

THE SILVER SCREEN

In 1937, during his run with the *Rhythm Review*, while working on Cole Porter's *Red Hot and Blue*, Hope was offered a part in *The Big Broadcast of 1938*, his first feature film. Hope's career in movies had not had a very promising beginning.

Bob: "Honey Chile, *where* are *you going* with that **mustard?**"

Honey: "You **never** know when you're going to **meet a ham.**"

Opposite: **Actress Clare Hazel and Bob Hope performed the Honey Chile routine Hope and Patricia Wilder had made famous on the *Rippling Rhythm Review* for NBC radio.** Left: **Hope records his *Pepsodent Radio Hour*. The successful formula of the show, which was built around Hope's monologue skills, kept the show on prime time until the demise of the radio variety show in the 1950s.**

The Many Memories

Bob Hope was not thrilled as he read through "Thanks for the Memory" when he arrived for work on the set of *The Big Broadcast of 1938*. For starters, it was a duet, and he had envisioned getting a solo number in the picture. Then there was the song itself. "Thanks for the Memory" was originally written to be an up-tempo number, but director Mitch Leisen decided to slow the song down and take the unusual step of recording it live for the film, rather than taping it and dubbing it in later. The power of the song came as a shock to everyone. According to legend, there wasn't a dry eye on the set as Hope and Shirley Ross finished the bittersweet song about a divorced couple reunited while strolling down memory lane. The song was interspersed with dialogue, which was where Hope found room in later years to update the number for various topical situations, making it an ideal all-purpose show-closing song.

The number became a minor hit, which the studio tried to capitalize on by pairing Hope and Ross in a light comedy titled *Thanks for the Memory* (1938). The song might have faded into obscurity if it hadn't been for Hope's radio show. Pepsodent was looking for a theme song for the show and had planned to use a line from "Wintergreen for President" by changing it to "Hope for Pepsodent," but the royalties for the Gershwin tune were too steep. Hope suggested he try "Thanks for the Memory" as a solo, talking his way through half the song; it became his trademark closing for every performance.

He had made his first appearance in Culver City in 1930 at Pathè Studios; he didn't make it past the screen test. "My nose entered the picture ten minutes before the rest of me," Hope said of the experience. It was true that cameras were less forgiving about his features than a live audience was, but his broad vaudeville acting techniques were not suitable for film. Hope cringed when remembering his early short comedies, which he made for a New York company called Educational Films. About a farce called *Going Spanish* (1934), he said, "We hopped around like Mexican jumping beans." He cracked to columnist Walter Winchell that if John Dillinger were ever caught, his punishment would be to sit through *Going Spanish* twice.

Hope was discouraged by his failure in films, but he brushed his disappointment off easily because, after all, he was a star of Broadway and the biggest vaudeville houses in the United States. He felt that his style of comedy simply wasn't appropriate for film. But the new offer was on a larger scale. Paramount Studios wanted him for the fourth *Big Broadcast* movie, and Hope could not refuse the opportunity to work with W.C. Fields, Dorothy Lamour, and Shirley Ross, among others. Like the other *Big Broadcast* movies, *The Big Broadcast of 1938* was really an extended musical-comedy variety show strung together with a silly plot. It is a farce about two ocean liners in a race across the Atlantic. W.C. Fields plays the owner of one of the ships, the USS *Gigantic*, while Hope plays Buzz Fielding, the emcee and disc jockey. Fielding places a bet that the *Gigantic* will win so that he can pay off his ex-wives, but along the way the ship runs into a spate of bad luck, brought on supposedly by the arrival of Fields' daughter, played by Martha Raye.

Hope and his wife reluctantly packed and left New York for Hollywood so that he could begin work on the film. Hope had been a star in New York, where he had played the Palace Theater and appeared on the radio every week, but he was a newcomer to Tinseltown.

Left: **Bob Hope and Shirley Ross bluff their way through a ventriloquist routine in his Hollywood film debut, *The Big Broadcast of 1938*. The plot was a lot of nonsense about two boats racing across the Atlantic, the real purpose of which was to showcase variety acts and Hope's talents as emcee.** Opposite: **Hope kicks up his heels with Martha Raye in *The Big Broadcast of 1938*.**

That Nose

The Big Broadcast of 1938 was responsible for a Hope trademark: the caricature profile drawing of his ski-slope nose. The movie posters and film titles had the entire cast drawn in profile caricature. Hope was so recognizable in the drawing that similar images of him were used in his future appearances. Ever the keen publicist, Hope latched on to the drawing, had it re-created by a commercial artist, and eventually copyrighted it.

Right: **W. C. Fields' big red honker and Martha Raye's big mouth were features so distinctive that they could easily be made into caricatures for advertising. Hope liked the idea, and after his ski-slope nose caricature was drawn for the ad campaign of *The Big Broadcast of 1938*, it became his trademark.**

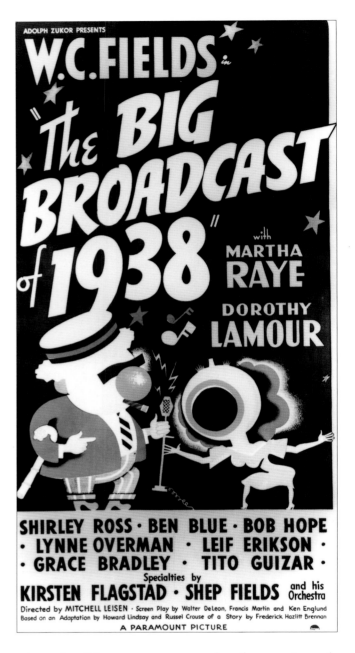

ADOLPH ZUKOR PRESENTS

W.C. FIELDS in

"The BIG BROADCAST of 1938"

with MARTHA RAYE

DOROTHY LAMOUR

SHIRLEY ROSS · BEN BLUE · BOB HOPE · LYNNE OVERMAN · LEIF ERIKSON · GRACE BRADLEY · TITO GUIZAR ·
Specialties by
KIRSTEN FLAGSTAD · SHEP FIELDS and his Orchestra
Directed by MITCHELL LEISEN · Screen Play by Walter DeLeon, Francis Martin and Ken Englund
Based on an Adaptation by Howard Lindsay and Russel Crouse of a Story by Frederick Hazlitt Brennan
A PARAMOUNT PICTURE

As Dolores set up house, she was dismayed to find that none of their new neighbors had ever heard of Bob Hope. But that soon changed: *The Big Broadcast of 1938* was a hit for Paramount Studios, as was Bob's musical duet with Shirley Ross, "Thanks for the Memory."

Hope began his feature film career playing a scene in alimony jail, where each of his three ex-wives and his current fiancée visit him to gloat and fight over their portion of his income. In early takes of the movie, Hope still had difficulty acting before the cameras. The studio was worried about his nose and suggested that rhinoplasty was in order. Hope was eager to do whatever it took to succeed in Hollywood, but Dolores refused, saying, "I like your face just the way it is." Hope suffered from the same problems that many stage actors have when trying to act on film for the first time: his actions were too big and his face seemed wooden as he spoke his lines. It wasn't until director Mitch Leisen told him to study Greta Garbo that Hope got the hang of movie acting.

Hope spent hours before a mirror studying his eye movements and allowing his face to read the emotions in the script. He also realized that his ski-slope nose was an asset, not a liability, because he could use it to get laughs. He stopped trying to camouflage his snout, much to the relief of Paramount's bewildered makeup artists. Hope relaxed a bit on the set and began to ease into his role in the film.

The best number in *The Big Broadcast of 1938* was "Thanks for the Memory." While the song launched the beginning of Hope's career as a film star, it serenaded the end of Fields'. *The Big Broadcast of 1938* was Fields' last feature film, and he managed to work in a silly golf game routine that had nothing to do with the rest of the movie. Ironically Hope did not participate in the scene—it was a passing of the putter of sorts, for after that, Hope took up the task of lampooning and popularizing golf in Hollywood. Bob Hope and Bing Crosby used golf as a publicity tool as early as 1937, when they played for the title of Golf Champion of the Entertainment World. The event made it into the papers, and Hope, the loser, had to work without compensation for one day on Bing Crosby's movie *Doctor Rhythm*.

COMMANDER OF THE AIRWAVES

Although his film career was beginning to take off, Hope still had a radio contract to complete with Woodbury, so he was forced to do the remainder of his shows from California. He was expected to tape his segments, which amounted to only a few minutes of airtime, while the bulk of the show would be broadcast from New York. Hope knew he could never find an audience for a few minutes of monologue and was desperate to have some reaction to his jokes. Luckily, he was assigned a studio adjacent to the much larger studio in which *The Edgar Bergen and Charlie McCarthy Show* was being produced. While the popular comic and his sidekick dummy warmed up the crowd, Bob and some of his staff rearranged the velvet ropes outside Bergen's studio. When the audience left, they dutifully followed the ropes into Hope's studio, where he entertained them briefly with his monologue.

Hope's shenanigans paid off, and he was offered his own show. He gave his name and talents to a weekly musical comedy hour sponsored by Pepsodent. Hope's Tuesday night show became a hit, with Bob hosting such stars as Judy Garland and Dorothy Lamour. Occasionally Bing Crosby would take time out from his own radio show to drop by Bob's, and Hope sometimes appeared on Crosby's show. The pair continued their on-air rivalry, filled with ad-libs and good-natured ribbing. As in earlier years, Bob made cracks about Bing being old, while Bing replied with jokes about Bob's nose. The insults flew until Crosby sang and Bob clowned around, upstaging the crooner. Bing waited to get his revenge until Bob was involved in a sketch with a female member of the cast, and then Bing would steal her attention away from Bob.

Hope and Shirley Ross, playing former spouses Buzz and Cleo Fielding in *The Big Broadcast of 1938*, display their dancing skills as well as their singing talents.

Bob Hope and Bing Crosby's long-term professional association and friendship began in vaudeville and was strengthened during their radio days. They would continue working together in movies and television until Crosby's death in 1977. Here they appear in *Road to Rio,* one of the many *Road* movies, as musicians Hot Lips Barton and Scat Sweeney.

Crosby, Hope, and Frank Sinatra worked closely together on the radio show *Command Performance* during World War II. Here, they horse around before a golf tournament in January 1944. Hope remarked that Sinatra was called a pin-up boy because "You had to pin him up or he'd fall over." Sinatra and Hope remained friends over the years, playing celebrity golf tournaments and benefit gigs.

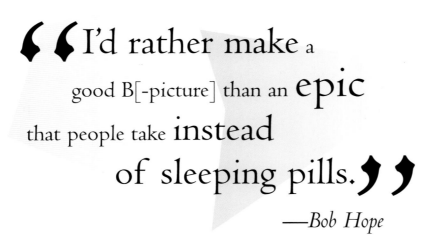

" I'd rather make a good B[-picture] than an **epic** that people take **instead** of sleeping pills. **"**

—*Bob Hope*

Although the atmosphere was spontaneous, the jokes were not. Hope had a team of writers to supply him and Crosby with enough so-called ad-libs to keep the audience in nonstop spasms of laughter.

Unlike vaudeville, where jokes and gags could be recycled for months or even years, radio required fresh material every week. The big radio names each had a team of writers, and Hope was no exception. Instead of the usual team of one or two, Hope hired as many as twelve writers at once to provide jokes. He was the first to admit this publicly, and it became a long-running joke on the show. Judy Garland once cracked that the writers "look like Notre Dame leaving the field for halftime." Hope's Army, as his writing team came to be called, was expected to produce reams of material. Hope called the writers together once a week and listened to them pitch their material. If a joke was good enough to crack up a room full of professionals, it was used; otherwise, it was relegated to the ever-growing filing cabinet of material Hope kept on hand for emergencies. Hope's Army became a talent pool for film and television for decades to come. One of his writers, Sherwood Schwartz, went on to create such 1970s classics as *The Brady Bunch* and *Gilligan's Island.*

Bob created the formula for the *Pepsodent Radio Hour,* and he used this formula throughout the show's enormously successful run. After an opening musical number by Skinnay Ennis and his orchestra, Bob came out and performed his monologue of topical humor. Then he introduced the guest star, usually a famous actress, and there would be a sketch involving Bob, the guest, and one of the regulars. Over the years his regulars included Jerry Colonna, the comic duo Brenda and Cobina, and Vera Vague. The sketch was followed by either the vocal group Six Hits and a Miss or a solo by one of the female singers who became star attractions to the show. The *Pepsodent Radio Hour* featured the talents of Judy Garland, Frances Langford,

Hope looks to his studio audience, waiting for their reaction to a joke, before continuing with a recording of his *Pepsodent Radio Hour*. To his left are frequent guests Jerry Colonna (standing) and Brenda Frazier (of the ditsy duo Brenda and Cobina).

Doris Day, and Gloria Jean. After the second musical number, Hope and his regulars ran another sketch, ending with his trademark "Thanks for the Memory."

THE FIRST TOUR OF DUTY

After the first season of the *Pepsodent Radio Hour*, Bob and Dolores took a much-needed vacation in Europe. They visited Bob's relatives, including his ninety-six-year-old grandfather, in England and were going to embark on a tour of the Continent, starting in Paris. But the Hopes were unexpectedly called home on August 25, 1939, by Paramount Studios, whose directors were nervous about having their valuable stars stranded in a potential war zone. The Hopes received word that the first shots of World War II had been fired as they were returning on the *Queen Mary*. The boat was crowded to full capacity with tourists who were cutting their vacations short and with Europeans fleeing the conflict. That night Hope was scheduled to entertain the grim, anxious crowd aboard the ship, but he was not looking forward to it. Just before they had left for Europe, Bob and Dolores had been told that they would be able to adopt a baby. Their excitement turned to anxiety as news of the war loomed. The Hopes, especially Dolores, were uncertain about starting a family in a time of war and even feared that they might not make it home safely to meet the baby.

When Bob went onstage that night, he turned the palpable tension around in his favor. He broke the ice by writing a few joke verses for "Thanks for the Memory," making references to the overcrowded conditions. "Thanks for the memory," Hope sang. "Some slept on the floor. Some in the corridor, but I was more exclusive, my room had 'Gentlemen' above the door."

The *Queen Mary* show was just a warm-up for the long road ahead, and the difficult circumstances must have seemed like a dream compared to the tough shows he played later in the war. As the war in Europe escalated, Hope began doing benefit shows at military bases around the country. He fell in love with military audiences, who were starved for entertainment and, especially, a glimpse of the beautiful women who were always onstage with him. He began broadcasting the *Pepsodent Radio Hour* from military bases, and after the United

Hope rehearses with his longtime sidekick, Jerry Colonna. Colonna appeared on Hope's radio show, toured with him during World War II and the Korean War, and even played bit parts in several of the *Road* pictures.

Opposite: **World War II was the first of many wars in which Hope was on the front lines as an entertainer. During the Korean War, Bob and Dolores Hope set off on tour together. Dolores toured with her husband's company, singing standards for homesick soldiers.**

States entered the war at the end of 1941, Hope began to appear regularly on the weekly radio show *Command Performance*, which was broadcast to the troops on Armed Forces Radio.

Hope was allowed to return to more risqué, vaudeville-type material because *Command Performance* was not broadcast stateside. He teased the soldiers into a frenzy by picking lint off Gypsy Rose Lee's sweater and saying, "How'd you like to have this patrol, fellas?" Stateside radio wouldn't have wanted Hope to even acknowledge that there was anything different or interesting about her sweater. But in combat, sex—at least the absence of it— was the biggest joke of all. One of Hope's favorite gags was, "You're not even allowed to think about girls here. At night the sergeant walks through and wakes up anybody with a smile on his face."

Above: **As the United States moved on to television, so did Hope, pictured here in 1953, toward the end of his radio days.**

Chapter 3

HOUSEHOLD NAME

With a little work, Hope transferred his comedic talents and ability to relate to an audience, which had made him a success in vaudeville and radio, to the big screen. Above: Bob Hope plays Sylvester the Great in *The Princess and the Pirate*, a movie about a hack actor who stows away on a pirate ship, pretending to be its salty captain. Opposite: In the movies, Hope occasionally, very occasionally, got to play the suave sophisticate with a sarong-wearing girl in every port. *Road to Singapore* was the only one of the many *Road* pictures, a series of films he did with Bing Crosby, in which Hope got the girl.

"If radio made me a star,"
Bob Hope said in his memoir
The Road to Hollywood, *"then*
movies made me a household name."

But immediately after the success of *The Big Broadcast of 1938,* Paramount was uncertain how to use Hope. It was clear that he was popular as the movie's emcee, but the part had originally been written for Jack Benny. So Paramount put Hope in the big production musical *College Swing* (1938), where he got lost amidst the shuffle of bigger stars such as George Burns and Gracie Allen.

After *College Swing,* the studio teamed Hope up with Martha Raye for a couple of comedies, *Give Me a Sailor* (1938) and *Never Say Die* (1939). In *Give Me a Sailor,* Hope plays a skirt-chasing sailor who falls for a dame, bombshell Betty Grable, who is clearly out of his league. After confusion and slapstick, Hope discovers he has affection for Grable's sister and sidekick, everywoman Martha Raye.

In *Never Say Die,* Hope benefited from the screenwriting talents of Preston Sturges, one of Paramount's greatest directors, who made such classics as *Unfaithfully Yours,* throughout the 1940s. Although the script was filled with Sturges' witty, quirky dialogue, it didn't provide much room for Hope's comic persona to shine through. Hope was best in active situations, where his cowardice was contrasted to the actions of other characters around him. In *Never Say Die,* Hope is a hypochondriac who is humored by those around him because he is rich, a part that could have been played by almost any of Paramount's leading men.

The first movie that was conceived specifically as a star vehicle for Hope was *Thanks for the Memory* (1938), the plot of which was built around the lyrics to the song. It was Hope's first chance to play a romantic lead, which was a novel turn of events for a comedian in Hollywood. Unfortunately, the script was thin on laughs, and the movie didn't do very well at the box office. Hope never forgot that lesson and from then on, no matter how good a part offered

to him was, he made sure it had enough laughs for him. At the very least, he demanded room for humorous situations so that his writers could punch up the script a bit.

Dolores and Bob permanently settled in the Toluca Lake section of Los Angeles, where Bob was making movies and taping the *Pepsodent Radio Hour*. The adoption of their first baby went through in 1939, and they brought home a baby girl whom they named Linda. Bob had wanted a boy, but he warmed to the baby when he saw how quickly Dolores became attached to her. A year later, they were called to the adoption agency again, this time to meet an infant boy who shared Bob's profile. "That little character with the ski-slide nose—that's for me," he said. The baby was named Anthony Hope—Tony for short.

ON THE ROAD

That same year Hope filmed the movie that made him a household name. The road to the making of *Road to Singapore* (1940) was itself a strange Hollywood tale of accidental fortune. Paramount had a script for a low-budget film called *Road to Mandalay,* a musical comedy set in

The classic All-American family: Bob, Dolores, and their older children, Tony and Linda, pose for a Hollywood photo opportunity with the cat and dog.

Above left: **Hope is dressed in a Bavarian hat and lederhosen as he climbs mountains near "Badgasswater" in *Never Say Die*. In the film, Hope's cowardly character, Mr. Kidley, is challenged to a duel by a Mr. Smirnoff, who says, "We meet at dawn at Dead Oaks." Mr. Kidley gets into Smirnoff's face as if angry and replies, suddenly chickening out, "I'm sure I'll never find the place."**
Above right: **Bob gets gardening tips from Martha Raye in *Give Me a Sailor*. Raye and Hope made three movies together in the late 1930s. She and Shirley Ross were Hope's first main leading ladies.**

an exotic location and featuring beautiful women in swimwear and plenty of silly situations. The studio approached George Burns and Gracie Allen first, but the husband-and-wife team turned down the movie because of their schedules. Paramount hired Frank Butler and Don Hartman to rework the script for two males instead of a couple, thinking that Jack Oakie and Fred MacMurray would play the leads. Eventually, the studio decided to capitalize on the chemistry that Bob Hope and Bing Crosby had developed during their collaboration in vaudeville and radio. Dorothy Lamour was added to the lineup as the woman for whom Hope and Crosby would compete, and suddenly the men's rivalry had a purpose.

Road to Singapore established a number of running gags that were used frequently throughout the six *Road* pictures that followed. One of the most memorable is the "pattycake punch," in which Hope and Crosby stand before the villain, who was often played by the ethnic chameleon Anthony Quinn. Hope and Crosby begin a pattycake that ends with both of them smacking Quinn straight on the kisser. *Road to Singapore* is the only *Road* movie in which Hope ends up winning the affections of the prized lady. In subsequent films, it's Crosby who ends up with the girl. Hope recalled in his book *The Road to Hollywood* that producer Harlan Thompson had said, "You get Lamour? Really, Mr. Hope, this is a comedy, not a fantasy." *Road to Singapore* is also the only *Road* movie in which Hope, not Crosby, is the instigator of all the trouble that occurs. After that, Hope is always the one to get fired from a cannon, sold

Above: **In what is perhaps the most famous still from his film career, Hope is clearly enjoying his short-lived victory of stealing Lamour away from Crosby. It is hard to tell which his character more enjoys—kissing Dottie or besting Bing.** Left: **Bob, Dottie, and Bing in the first *Road* movie, *Road to Singapore*. Here Bob "helps" Dottie with the guitar.**

Bing on Bob

Bing Crosby was Bob Hope's on-screen rival, golf nemesis, frequent business partner, and longtime friend. Although their relationship appeared to be founded on rivalry, Bing gave up his usual cracks about Bob's "ski nose" and "shovel head" when he wrote a letter to *Time* magazine in rebuttal to its allegation that Bob Hope was cheap. "My friend, Bob Hope," Crosby began, "is anything but cheap. He does an average of two benefits per week. His fee for a personal appearance would be about $10,000, so he gives away $20,000 every week of his life. Is that cheap?" It was a rare admission of friendship for Bing, especially in his ever-sparring relationship with Bob. Hope and Crosby continued to make public appearances together until Bing retired and moved to northern California shortly before his death in 1977.

"Paramount realized I was very stubborn and that I was going to stay in show business regardless of my talents. So they decided to give me a chance to play opposite Shirley Ross, who requested that I play as far opposite as possible."

—*Bob Hope*

into slavery, or sent deep-sea diving, while Crosby collects his paycheck and a kiss from Dorothy Lamour. Bob often evened the score by undercutting Bing's musical number with a crack such as, "He's gonna sing, folks; now's the time to go out and get popcorn."

Road to Singapore was a fairly formulaic comedy with an above-average script, but what made it and all the other *Road* movies stand out was the feeling of ad-libbed breeziness that Hope and Crosby brought to the set. It seems to the viewer that the actors are just making up their lines as they go along, when in reality the ad-libs were written by Hope's writing team (though they were never actually put into Butler and Hartman's scripts). Hope knew that the key to the ad-lib isn't what you say, but how and when you say it. As Hope said about Don Rickles' ad-lib "Well, the war must be over," when Bob caught his act on *The Dean Martin Show* in 1973, "Timing shows more in ad-libs than anything else." And Bob's timing in the *Road* movies is as close as he ever came to putting his rapport with an audience into a feature film. The live feel might be attributable to the audience of Hollywood stars who came just to watch the *Road* movies being filmed. Stars such as Cary Grant and Humphrey Bogart dropped by the set in the hopes of getting a cameo or just to enjoy the jokes.

The director of *Road to Singapore,* Victor Scherzinger, was irritated at first by Hope and Crosby's disregard for the rules, but eventually he gave up trying to find his place in the script, quipping, "You know, I really shouldn't take any money for this job. All I do is say 'Stop' and 'Go.'" Dorothy Lamour missed her cues on account of Hope and Crosby's shenanigans and was irritated by their devil-may-care attitude—until she got used to Bob and Bing. Word spread quickly about the fun-loving atmosphere on the set, and soon veteran Hollywood crew members were fighting to be part of the next picture, *Road to Zanzibar* (1941).

Bob and Bing strut their stuff alongside the ladies' chorus in *Road to Zanzibar*.

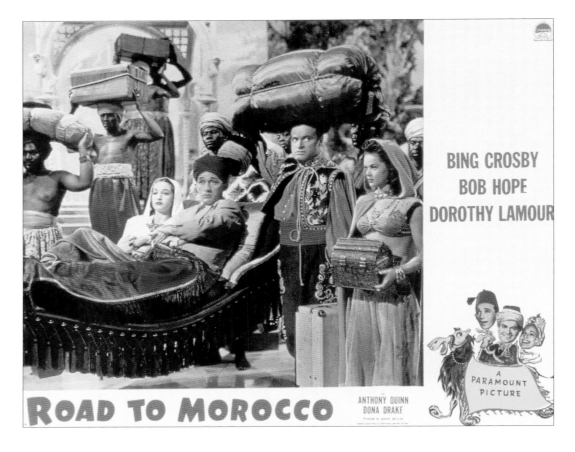

The *Road* movies were widely publicized and incredibly popular around the world. Each movie featured beautiful women, exotic locales, and of course, Bob, Bing and Dottie. Above left: **The Belgian poster for *Road to Zanzibar* featured Crosby and Hope ogling "sarong girl" Lamour.** Above right: **Bing bests Bob at the end of *Road to Morocco*. Right: Bing and Bob earn their passage in *Road to Utopia* by swabbing the poopdeck.** The pair was always in some sort of down-and-out, perilous circumstance. There was danger, but it was cartoonish, and you never believed any harm would come to either of them because, as Hope points out early in *Road to Rio* as he's dangling from a tightrope, "The picture would be over right now." It is not difficult to see how audiences during World War II and its aftermath appreciated comedy that was set in some vague bygone era when traveling the world was a light-hearted adventure.

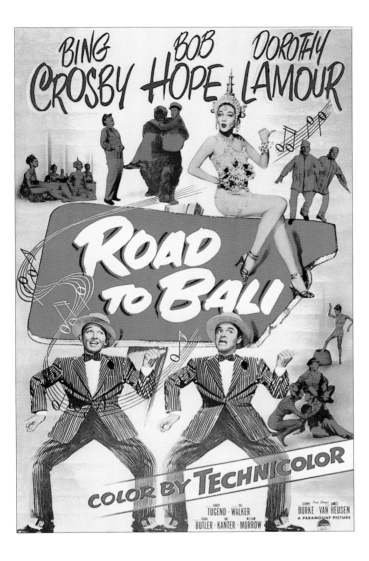

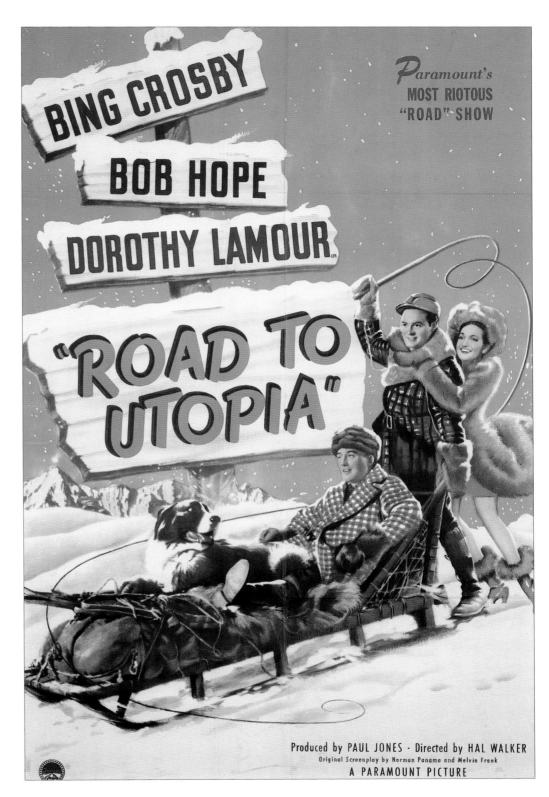

Above: **Bob and Bing dressed as vaudevillians for this** *Road to Bali* **poster. In the film, they act out an old vaudeville routine revived from Hope's days with Lefty Durbin.** Right: *Road to Utopia* **saw Bob and Bing transferred way up North. Perhaps** *Road* **writers Frank Butler and Don Hartman had exhausted their extensive repertoire of tropical humor.**

Bob Hope, as Hot Lips Barton, and Bing Crosby, as Scat Sweeney, came together again in *Road to Rio*. They were always down-on-their-luck actors, singers, dancers, or in this case, jazz musicians. They are clearly out of their league in the glamorous hot spots of Rio.

Occasionally the *Road* antics got out of hand. During the filming of *Road to Utopia*, Hope and Crosby skipped a day's shooting to play golf. They didn't bother to inform the studio that they were playing hooky, and Lamour was left waiting in a period evening gown for six hours. She had to be propped against a special leaning board that actresses used for corseted costumes. Eventually Gary Cooper dropped by and talked her into changing out of her costume for the rest of the day. She had just removed the uncomfortable ensemble when Bing and Bob arrived ready to work. They apologized but jokingly referred to her as "that temperamental Dottie who walked off the set."

Hope's gags were fresh and sounded modern, especially when placed in the timeless context of the *Road* movies. There were references to studio contracts, politics, and Crosby's hobbies, including horse racing. The duo was not afraid to break the fourth wall, the invisible

barrier between performer and audience, by admitting that this was just a movie; there are dozens of examples of inside jokes in the *Road* pictures. After a long speech in which Hope recaps the plot of *Road to Morocco* (1942) during the movie itself, Bing snaps, "I know all that." Bob argues, "But the people who came in the middle of the picture don't," to which Bing replies, suddenly concerned, "Really? Ya think they missed my song?" At one point in *Road to Rio* (1947), Hope and Crosby hide in a meat locker and find a side of beef that has been stamped by Crosby Stables.

The *Road* pictures used the most current special effects to enhance old vaudeville jokes. In *Road to Morocco,* Hope is sassed by talking camels, and in *Road to Bali* (1952), animation is used to put Hope's face on a chimpanzee, with somewhat eerie results. One of the most clever special effects was a simple misdubbing of voices in *Road to Morocco.* Hope, Crosby, and Lamour took turns singing the verses of the song, and the voice track was dubbed along with the wrong lip-synched visual. Bob serenades Dorothy with her own voice, Bing croons to Bob with Dorothy's voice, and Bob and Bing sing to each other with their voices reversed.

Bob and Bing in the first *Road* picture, *Road to Singapore*. Songs, South Seas senoritas, and silliness were the keys to the film's success. The basic formula was repeated for the remaining movies. *Road to Singapore* made Bob a household name, as Hope himself cracked, "like Sani-flush."

Above: **Bob proves he coulda been a contender. As host of the 1954 Academy Awards, Hope pretended to fight Marlon Brando for the latter's Best Actor Oscar for On the Waterfront.** Opposite: **Hope always made a joke of the fact that he never won an Oscar during his many years as Academy Awards emcee.**

ON HIS OWN

Road to Singapore was a smash hit that propelled Hope to stardom. He had been one of several emcees at the Oscars the year before, but the Academy took note of his sudden popularity and began the tradition of having a single host for the big event. The 1939 Oscar ceremony, held in March 1940, was the most spectacular in the history of Hollywood. In what was dubbed "Hollywood's golden year," Hope presided over the ceremony in which *Gone with the Wind, Wuthering Heights, Mr. Smith Goes to Washington, The Wizard of Oz, Goodbye Mr. Chips, Dark Victory,* and *Of Mice and Men* competed for Best Picture. Until 1940, the winners of the Academy Awards were announced in advance, and the awards were presented at a dinner. Since everyone knew upon arriving at the ceremony that *Gone with the Wind* had swept the Oscars with an unprecedented eight awards, Hope started the evening by announcing, "What a wonderful thing, this benefit for [*Gone with the Wind* producer] David O. Selznik." Bob also presented a special Screen Juvenile Oscar to Judy Garland, who had recently become a regular cast member on Hope's *Pepsodent Hour* radio show.

Although he presided over the ceremony for ten years, Hope never won an acting Oscar. He has been presented with five honorary Academy Awards for his service as an emcee

Above: **Bob Hope and the great comedienne Lucille Ball as Sorrowful Jones and Gladys O'Neill in their first movie together, *Sorrowful Jones*. The film also stars the criminally cute Mary Jane Saunders as Martha Smith, whom Jones acquires as a marker for a gambling debt.**

Opposite, left: **Bob Hope sneaks out of his army medical exam in *Caught in the Draft*. The film deals with the serious issue of the draft in a comic way, examining the lighter side of conscription.** Opposite, right: **Hope looks dapper for *Fancy Pants*, the musical remake of *Ruggles of Red Gap*, the story of a butler who tries to tame a family in the Wild West.**

and for his humanitarian efforts. In *Road to Bali*, he jokes about losing at the Oscars. While escaping a swamp full of alligators, Hope bumps into Humphrey Bogart—in costume for *The African Queen*, pulling a boat through the muck. After his short cameo, Bogart disappears quickly and Crosby calls after him, "Bogie, wait, you forgot your Oscar." Hope quickly snatches away the much coveted golden statue, saying, "Give it here, you've already got one," referring to Crosby's Best Actor win for *Going My Way* in 1945.

Shortly after joining Paramount, Bob became dissatisfied with the studio's publicity staff and hired his own publicist, Mack Millar. This was an unusual step, as one of the supposed advantages of working for a studio was the factory system in which publicity and writing were something the actors needn't worry about.

One of Millar's first tasks was to help Hope cross over from the movies and work sketches from *Road to Singapore* into the *Pepsodent Radio Hour*. As easily as he'd used radio to promote his vaudeville act, Hope used his own radio show to further his film career. If actors did today what Hope did in the 1940s, they would suffer from overexposure and the public would tire of them, but Hope wore well. He was never so strong a personality

that he became annoying. It was this, as *Time* magazine put it, "vibrant averageness" that kept him at the top of every medium in which he appeared. Millar put Hope in radio sketches based on the film to announce that it was opening soon. It wasn't long before Hope and Crosby were back in the studio working with Scherzinger on *Road to Zanzibar*. The original script had called for Hope's character, Fearless Frazier, to again be the instigator of trouble, but Scherzinger decided that the chemistry worked better with Crosby as the troublemaker and Hope the hapless victim.

The *Road* movies were examples of unapologetic escapism, but Paramount planned something a bit more serious for Hope's next film, *Caught in the Draft* (1941). With war approaching, the topic was weighty for a comedy. Hope's wisecracking, cowardly character perfectly fit the part of Don Bolton, a yellow-bellied film actor who enlists in the army in order to win a general's daughter, played by Dorothy Lamour. After shooting was completed, Hope was invited to do a show at March Field, a flight training base in southern California, as a publicity stunt to promote the movie. He did his first GI-oriented broadcast on the *Pepsodent Radio Hour* on May 6, 1941. His entire

He's a hilarious hawkshaw...with a case on Dottie!

BOB HOPE and DOROTHY LAMOUR in

"My Favorite Brunette"

with PETER LORRE LON CHANEY

Produced by Daniel Dare
Directed by Elliott Nugent
A Paramount Release

opening monologue was adapted to fit his audience, and the crowd was incredibly responsive, although Hope was characteristically humble about it: "What a welcome I received—a ten-gun salute, they told me on the operating table." The success of the March Field broadcast coupled with the timeliness of the subject matter made *Caught in the Draft* Hope's biggest hit to date without Crosby. It also proved to Paramount that Bob Hope could carry a picture.

BOB AND DOTTIE

The Hope-Lamour pairing in *Caught in the Draft* was almost as successful as the Hope-Crosby-Lamour team had been in the *Road* movies. Hope was paired with her two more times without Crosby—in *They Got Me Covered* (1943), a spy-thriller spoof about a reporter who becomes entangled in an international web of intrigue, and in *My Favorite Brunette* (1947), a detective spoof about a baby photographer who gets entangled in an international web of intrigue. In *My Favorite Brunette*, Alan Ladd, Peter Lorre, and Lon Chaney perform as though they are in a serious film noir. In contrast, Hope behaves like his usual self, as though he's in a Daffy Duck cartoon—drinking tough-guy bourbon that knocks him out after one sip and cracking a stream of one-liners from death row.

Bob and Dottie, as Hope called her, worked out a routine that became a mainstay in the Hope persona. At the end of *Caught in the Draft,* Hope needs to warn his fellow unit soldiers, who are out on war games, that they are wandering onto the artillery range. He is unable to overcome his fear until Lamour rushes out into artillery fire to do his job for him. At one point in the fracas, a gun goes off and he leaps into her arms. This strong woman/weak man joke was the basis for almost all of the comedy in *Paleface* (1948) and *Fancy Pants* (1950), in which Bob was paired with competent women—Jane Russell and Lucille Ball, respectively—in order to exaggerate his cowardly manner.

VERSATILE FLAIR

Although Hope was famous for his comedy, Paramount gave him the lead in a glitzy Technicolor film version of Irving Berlin's stage musical *Louisiana Purchase* (1941). Hope plays a crooked New Orleans politician, Jim Taylor, who takes the fall for a gang of grifters. He has no solo musical numbers, yet he manages to inject his persona and his brand of hip, timely comedy into nearly all his scenes. He makes numerous references to President Franklin D. Roosevelt and does a wonderful *Mr. Smith Goes to Washington* parody when his character turns a plea for innocence into a filibuster. He begins reading in the Louisiana State Senate until Senator Loganberry, played by Victor Moore, protests, "You can't do this."

Hope replies, "Yes I can. I got special permission from Jimmy Stewart."

Hope's versatility with music, comedy, and dance gave him a wider choice of roles and allowed for a bit of variety in his comedies. Hope and Crosby play wandering vaudevillians in *Road to Bali*; the movie gave them an excuse to perform together onstage and recycle one of Bob's old vaudeville dance routines. In *Road to Rio*, Bob and Bing dress in drag for a musical number in which Bob sports Carmen Miranda–style fruit headgear in a slapstick parody of her hit "South American Way." Hope often used his musical ability to get laughs. One of the highlights of *Paleface* is the scene in which Hope serenades a disinterested Jane Russell with his squeeze-box version of "Buttons and Bows." The pair are traveling by wagon, and Hope pretends that the bumps in the road are causing his voice to skip like a record—a remarkable example of Hope's talent as both a singer and a comedian.

Throughout the late 1940s and 1950s, Hope found ways to fit his wisecracking persona into a variety of starring roles, as in the swashbuckling spoof *The Princess and the Pirate* (1944). In this parody of the type of period adventure Errol Flynn made famous, Hope plays Sylvester the Great, a hack actor who winds up impersonating a pirate captain. In a surreal twist, Bing Crosby appears in the last scene to steal Virginia Mayo from Hope, making the whole picture seem like an extended *Road* movie gag. When he wasn't spoofing familiar film genres, Hope occasionally appeared in straightforward comedies, such as *The Lemon Drop Kid* (1951), which was adapted from the Damon Runyon story of the same name.

Above: **Victor Moore, Bob Hope, and Vera Zorina in *Louisiana Purchase*. In this scene, Jim Taylor (Hope) disguises himself as a waiter to get Senator Loganberry (Moore) drunk. He tells the teetotaling senator that the gin is actually Mississippi River water.**
Opposite: **A publicity poster for *My Favorite Brunette* promises the audience plenty of brunettes from which to choose.**

THE SEVEN LITTLE FOYS

In no movie did Hope demonstrate his singing and dancing abilities more capably than in *The Seven Little Foys* (1955), which is one of the few films in which he does not play his cowardly character, but rather plays real-life vaudevillian Eddie Foy. The story follows Foy's struggles to create an act around his family after his wife dies. In one scene, Foy meets George M. Cohan at a banquet and the two get into a tap-dancing duel on top of the table. Paramount executives were hard-pressed to find an actor to play Cohan, since they wanted a recognizable name for walk-on pay and the role required considerable talent. James Cagney, then under contract to Warner Bros., volunteered to play the part since he'd known Foy when the vaudevillian was a struggling actor on Broadway. The tap-dancing scene turned out to be a highlight of the film, with Hope revealing his skills as a dancer, holding his own and occasionally surpassing Cagney.

The Seven Little Foys is probably Hope's high-water mark as an actor. The story is often serious, as he portrays a character dealing with the death of his wife. At one point Foy goes before a judge to plead for custody of his children. A similar scene had scored a Best Actor Oscar nomination for Cary Grant in *Penny Serenade,* but the role did not do the same for Hope. He had to settle for being a box-office sensation and a beloved personality. Hope had wonderful chemistry with the child actors who played the seven little Foys, and the scenes of him manhandling them through their act are charming and hilarious. Audiences loved the movie for its family fare at a time when James Dean was questioning traditional values in *East of Eden* and Frank Sinatra was portraying a heroin addict in *The Man with the Golden Arm.*

Bob Hope plays vaudevillian Eddie Foy in the biographical *Seven Little Foys*, which depicts the life of a widower who puts his family to work on stage.

Hope's heyday as a film star was in the 1940s and early 1950s. Sensibilities were changing in the United States in the late 1950s and 1960s, and as Cary Grant noted, "It was the era of blue jeans, the Method [Acting], and dope. Nobody wanted to do comedy." Hollywood was beginning to see the first rumblings of the counterculture that would give Hope so much trouble in his later years. Hope was inextricably linked to the older generation of stars, partly because of his experiences in World War II. But the waning of his star in Hollywood did not mean that his career was winding down. With his dedication to entertaining U.S. servicemen and -women around the world and his interest in the new medium of television, Bob Hope was more popular than ever.

THE
ROAD
TO...

Above: **Bob Hope was the embodiment of what John Steinbeck called the "clown hero" of World War II.** Opposite: **Hope wore many hats over the years, but his distinctive profile always stood out, whether he was appearing in the *Road* movies, in uniform entertaining the troops, or in Russia as an early Cold War ambassador of comedy.**

In 1996, Republican senator Bob Stump of Arizona corrected an oversight: he introduced a bill to Congress that made Bob Hope an honorary veteran of World War II.

The bill recognized the fact that Hope, who told jokes day after day in a raincoat and a flak helmet, was as important to morale and the war effort as he would have been had he actually enlisted in the service. When the air force wanted to give him rank, the other branches of the military protested, offering rank of their own and trying to outbid the air force in order to have the right to say he was theirs. But Hope belonged to all the branches of service in all the Allied countries of World War II. In addition to his acts for the U.S. armed forces, he performed for thousands of English soldiers during the Blitz and for the French after liberation.

During World War II, Hope returned to vaudeville, this time as the leading master of ceremonies for a traveling troupe of singers, comedians, and variety acts that entertained Allied soldiers around the world. Bob's penchant for doing benefit gigs during the Great Depression developed into a traveling show for the troops during the war. He played up to four shows a day throughout Europe, Africa, and the Pacific, entertaining hundreds of thousands of troops. In his memoir *I Never Left Home*, he joked, "Nowadays vaudeville comes with bullets. It used to be the other way around." Hope, like other movie stars, put his career on hold for the cause, but found that it provided him with invaluable exposure and terrific PR.

HOPE'S FIRST TOUR OF DUTY

After his first experience at March Field, a military base in southern California where he played before an air force crowd in 1941, Hope said, "How long has this been going on?" referring to the amazing response he got to his jokes. Hope found the traveling life exhilarating. After all, he was a vaudevillian at heart, and this new kind of vaudeville had some advantages over the old—the audiences were almost always appreciative, and the sleeping quarters were no longer segregated by sex. The performers lived in dangerous, uncomfortable condi-

tions, but Hope always looked at it as fun, often to the bewilderment of his fellow entertainers. He joked about every possible hardship, from food rationing to the lack of clean water for laundry. In *I Never Left Home,* he said, "I once met a man in England who owned an egg outright. He let me see it in his safe." Upon return from his first tour of war-torn Europe in 1943, Hope said, "Laundry? Forget about it. Yeah, sure you can sometimes find someone to do it for you, if you're willing to pay the price. That's how I made expenses."

Hope realized that he'd found his public: his audience was enthusiastic, large, and extremely informal. At one point during his first tour of England in 1943, a tank drove through the middle of the crowd, bringing the opening number to a halt. Everyone parted ways and watched the tank attentively until the driver appeared and stole the show by saying, "Okay, you can start the show now; I'm here." Hope loved these types of situations because they were perfectly suited to his breezy style of comedy. He'd say to the soldiers, "It's true I wore a dress in the *Road to Rio.*" Then he'd look one soldier in the eye and say, as if it had just occurred to him, "Don't laugh. If you'd have thought of it you wouldn't be here right now."

He told jokes at an astounding rate—six per minute—but the biggest laughs came from his reactions to his own jokes. "This is Bob *Command Performance* Hope here," he began,

Frances Langford and Bob Hope load a 90mm cannon near Tunis in 1944. Shortly after this photo was taken, Langford became the first woman to fire a gun of this size.

> ## " If I hadn't gone, I'd never have been able to look at myself in the mirror. "
> —*Bob Hope on his extraordinary service entertaining the troops in World War II*

Above: **Bob Hope stands at the microphone in 1969 on his annual Christmas USO tour. Unable to decide which trouble spot to visit, Hope circled the globe and played every place where troops were stationed.** Opposite: **Bob Hope shares some of his livelier memories with the troops for his television special, "Bob Hope Remembers World War II" in 1989.**

"telling every Nazi in Russia that Crimea doesn't pay." While the line received some laughter, Hope got an even bigger laugh when he rolled his eyes at his own corny pun. Then he paused briefly and said, "I'm now getting my material from [radio announcer] H.V. Kaltenborn," which got a tremendous laugh because the seemingly spontaneous joke referred to the Dan Rather of that era as just another of Hope's writers. This second joke was also scripted but told in a style that made it seem spontaneous. This appearance of spontaneity was the secret behind the *Road* movies, and it was equally as successful before GI audiences.

Bob Hope's style caught on, and soon he was leading Hollywood in the new frontier of military entertainment. He started catch phrases that became so popular in the European Theater of Operations that they often preceded his arrival. He showed up onstage and yelled, "Hiya, tourists!" and the soldiers shouted it with him. He was often playing in rather bleak, dull circumstances. As John Steinbeck noted of Hope in a 1943 article in the New York *Herald-Tribune*, "They feel forgotten but then they hear Hope is coming and they feel remembered."

HOPE AND COMPANY

Jokes were the raw material that fueled Hope's act on the road throughout England, Morocco, Italy, and Algiers. And with four shows a day, he needed lots of jokes. He'd phone his army of writers, on call for gag emergencies at all hours, forgetting transatlantic time differences and demanding jokes about a certain general, politician, or topographical location. While the writers supplied the punch lines, Hope peppered his jokes with the local army lingo, as Lieutenant John D. Saint, who served in the recently liberated Sicily, wrote in a letter home: "He can tell you about Lister bags, Atabrine tablets, and armor artificers. That made his comments much funnier to us. He was speaking our language."

Hope also found that by hiring enlisted man Jack Pepper as a replacement for Jerry Colonna, he could reach the men with one of their own. Hope met Pepper as a buck private who rushed up to greet the comedian after a show. Hope was amused by Private Pepper and hired him to fill in for Colonna on the tour since the mustachioed sidekick was too booked with other commitments to join him. Bandleader Tony Roma provided the music.

Hope's other longtime traveling companion, Frances Langford, said that Bob was like a GI himself. His whole operation moved like a military unit through combat zones and frequently took fire. Although there was supposed to be a gentleman's agreement preventing the enemy from firing on noncombatant planes, Hope joked grimly to Dolores before leaving the States, "Everyone knows the agreement isn't worth the gentleman it was written by."

Hope established a rapport with Langford while touring England, as well as a certain style that was repeated over the years with various beauties. He introduced her as "what you're fighting for," and Langford came out and teased the mostly male audience. "Our purpose on the tour was to be looked at," said Janis Page, who worked with Hope in Vietnam, "but I never felt like an object." Langford, Page, and the other women Hope brought on tour were not burlesque, but wholesome. Langford dressed scantily, but remarkably plainly, in khaki shorts and a halter top that revealed her belly. She was the all-American beauty playing war, and the GIs went crazy for her. During the closing number of "Thanks for the Memory," she sang, "I'd like to kiss each and every one of you," while Bob interrupted, "Do you want to get us trampled to death?" At the end of every show, one soldier was brought onstage for a dance and a kiss from Langford. The audience knew this ahead of time, which whipped them into a frenzy of enthusiasm, since each man hoped to be the one who got picked.

Phyllis on Bob

During Bob's tour of Vietnam, Phyllis Diller was called in to replace an ailing Jerry Colonna. "Bob taught me how to manage those hospital visits," she said. "The first one we went to I dissolved into tears and actually was no good at all. It was very dangerous, but I don't think he was a man who worried about death."

TOLLS OF WAR

While Bob pretended that the greatest dangers he faced were sex-starved soldiers trying to get a better look at Langford, he was living and working in and near combat zones. He was in a devastating air raid in Algiers that never ceased to haunt him. He and his Hollywood gypsies were staying in a hotel only a few blocks from the docks that became the target of a Nazi bomb raid. Hope found himself frozen in terror as flak flew by his window and crashing airplanes pockmarked the walls with machine-gun fire. He said later that the noise scared him so badly that the first thing he did when it ended was throw up. "I don't know how our boys stand it day after day," he marveled. He was so honest and sincere about his own fear that he provided a powerful link for people back home, who could only imagine what their loved ones were experiencing.

Hope's schedule took its toll on his personal life. As he was about to depart for England in 1943, his daughter Linda wished him "Goodbye, Bob Hope," as if she recognized him as a celebrity first and a father second. After his experience in Algiers, Bob was shaken; his first thoughts were about Dolores and the fact that he should have said something more than "I'll take care of myself" before he'd left her in California.

On that first tour of duty in 1943, Hope visited every hospital in his path, witnessing such horrors as tank operators who'd been burned over 90 percent of their bodies. Hope joked with these men, sat on their cots, and provided comfort in his own way. He reported about these men matter-of-factly in his memoirs, praising their bravery and high spirits in the face of their terrible sacrifice. Hope also faced the harsh reality that laughter could not help every wounded soldier. In *I Never Left Home*, he described playing a show in Exeter, England, before several hundred men with "advanced cases of war fatigue." Hope remembered the eerie audience response, saying: "We got very few laughs. And those we did get were in funny places and scattered. I mean there were absolutely no spots where the whole audience roared out together. . . . It was one of the hardest jobs I think I've ever done in my life to stay on that stage."

When Bob returned home from Europe in 1943, it was to a public that regarded him with much greater esteem than when he'd left. Of all the performers who'd pitched in to help the cause, Hope had gone farthest into the frontier and returned to tell the press of the job that American GIs were doing around the world. Hope seemed to be born to lead a traveling variety show. The Steinbeck article was syndicated throughout the American press, and Hope suddenly went from being a comic to a "clown hero in greasepaint." Steinbeck wrote, "It is impossible to see how he can do so much, can cover so much ground, can work so hard and be so effective. There's a man. There really is a man."

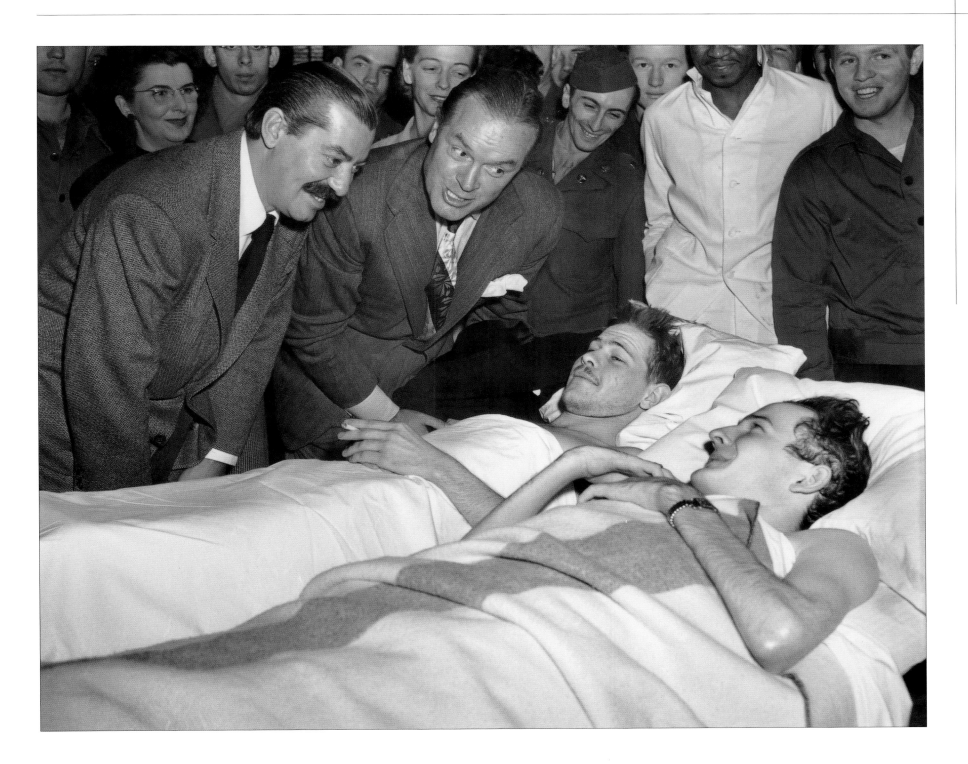

Hope and Jerry Colonna visit Private Charles Brown and P. F. C. Ben Collins at Walter Reed Hospital in Washington, D.C., in 1948. "Don't get up," Hope would always joke with those too sick to stand for his visit.

Bob Hope was famous for being able to cheer up just about anyone. While the hospital visits frequently got to other members of his company, including comedienne Martha Raye, who recalled bawling her eyes out after her visit to a hospital ward. Here, Hope chides a former POW in 1950 about his weight.

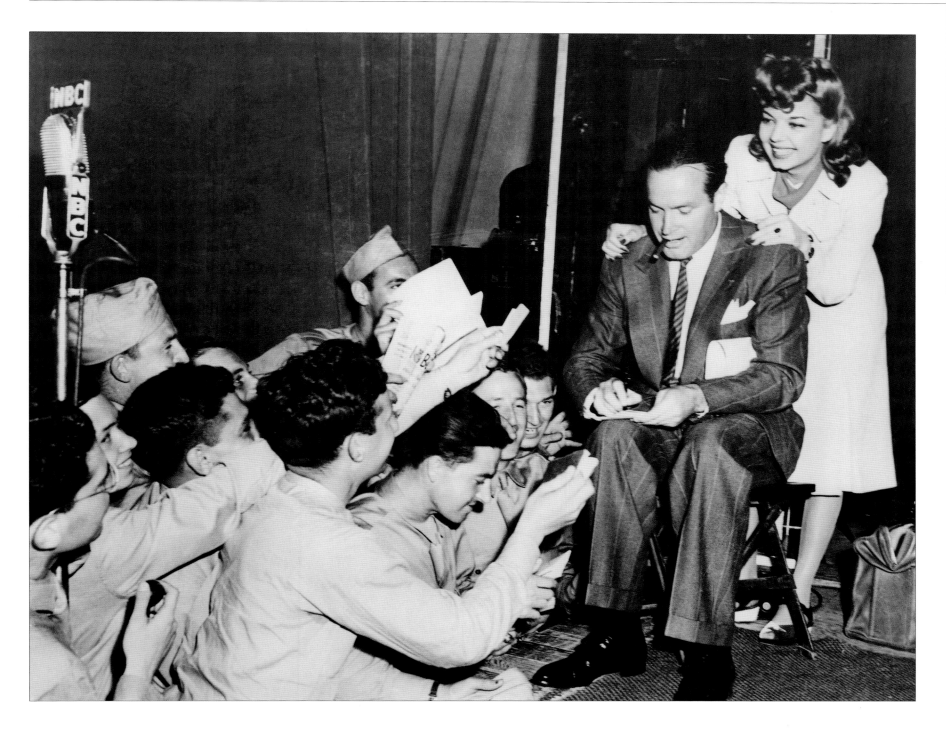

After World War II ended, Hope continued to devote a large amount of his time to performing for the armed forces, first in liberated Europe and then in Korea. Here, Hope and Frances Langford sign autographs for a GI audience in 1953.

Above: **Bob with Dolores, Tony, and Linda on the set of *Where There's Life* (1946). Bob used the occasion to get in a shot at Bing, saying, "That guy Crosby isn't the only handsome movie star with kids."** Opposite: **Bob and Dolores in 1948, between wars, when Bob was home to be with his family. His commitment to the troops meant that his wife and children often had to make do without him at Christmas and other holidays.**

Hope was committed to entertaining the troops, and no sooner did he return stateside from Italy and Africa than he was planning a tour of the Pacific. He prepared for the heat by playing some shows at training bases in the Caribbean. Jerry Colonna (who was free this time), Langford, and Tony Roma joined Bob on the trip. They played the usual Hope schedule of four shows a day throughout the summer of 1944 in the Marshall Islands and through the war-torn Pacific Atolls, bringing cheer to soldiers whose time spent in the South Pacific was anything but idyllic. At Noemfoor Island, the army brought down a Japanese fighter just twelve hundred yards (1,097m) from the stage. Despite Hope and his group's proximity to heavy combat, their closest scare came while they were headed to Australia for a break. Their plane was forced down in the Pacific on account of mechanical difficulties, and local Australians rescued them with small boats after they bailed out. In gratitude, Hope forgot about his relaxation and played a couple of shows in Sydney.

PEACE

After Victory in Europe Day, Hope took his troupe on a tour through Europe that ended in liberated France. It was a celebratory, festive occasion that came weeks before victory in Japan and the end of the war. Hope's chief uncertainty was how he was going to return to civilian life. As it turned out, he didn't have to worry. He filled in the short gap between the end of World War II and the Cold War by crisscrossing the United States when he wasn't making movies or doing his radio show. Hope played to veterans of the war who were now battling shortages and unemployment instead of the Axis powers. He was forced to readjust his *Pepsodent Radio Hour* for peacetime, toning down some of the racier routines

he did for *Command Performance.* He also had to readjust to playing before a studio of three hundred rather than thousands of boisterous servicemen.

But peace did not mean that Hope slowed down his workaholic pace. In 1945 he was invited to entertain Harry Truman and his family at the White House. He began writing a syndicated daily newspaper humor column called "It Says Here." Like his forerunner, Will Rogers, Hope was able to joke about politics because of his personal relationship with the President. As usual, Hope put his writers to work on "It Says Here," picking a topic and editing their jokes. He hosted the 1944 Oscars and watched Bing Crosby win Best Actor for *Going My Way.* Crosby accidentally picked up Ingrid Bergman's *Gaslight* Oscar from the table, and as they were sorting out the mistake, Hope ad-libbed, "Wouldn't it be wonderful if there was one left over?"

WARMTH IN THE COLD WAR

By 1948, the Cold War was heating up and Hope was sent to Germany to entertain the troops who were performing the Berlin Airlift. His show on Christmas Eve in Berlin highlighted the animosity between the Russians and Americans, who'd been Allies just three years prior. While Hope was a staunch supporter of the troops and U.S. anti-Communist foreign policy in general, he was not a fan of Red-baiter Joseph McCarthy. While Hope was doing political material in his newspaper column, his broadcasts became even more political as he formed a personal relationship with President Eisenhower, who was also a fellow golf fanatic. Eisenhower was scared of McCarthyism, and Hope allowed his writers to write a few anti-McCarthy jokes for his Colgate television show in 1952. "Senator McCarthy got off the train in Washington, D.C., and spent two days investigating redcaps," Hope joked.

Hope decided it would be good publicity to premier *Paris Holiday* (1958) in Moscow and do a broadcast there as a goodwill gesture during the Cold War. He had been fascinated with the idea of doing a show behind the Iron Curtain ever since MGM was refused the right to film his comedy *The Iron Petticoat* (1956) there. Hope doggedly pursued the Russian consulate until he was finally allowed permission to do the broadcast. He managed to adapt his jokes to a Russian audience by injecting topics into his act that both Russians and Americans would understand. "How about that vodka?" Hope asked the audience at the Spasso Theater in Moscow. "No wonder you got your *Sputnik* up there first. I'm surprised the whole country isn't up there with it." Hope closed his Moscow show with a serious plea for peace and mutual understanding.

President Harry Truman presents Bob with a scroll signed by more than a million GIs thanking Hope for his service during World War II.

GOOD MORNING, VIETNAM

Hope continued to tour all throughout Korea and Vietnam, often filming his shows for television and having them broadcast back in the States. Television audiences tuned in, trying to catch a glimpse of a relative in the crowd. Hope stuck to his rigorous schedule of up to four shows a day in combat areas even though he was in his sixties when he and his troup set out for Saigon.

Hope's first tour of duty in Vietnam was well received back home and with the soldiers. Greg Hegi, then a private first class with the First Cavalry Infantry Unit in Bonsoon, caught one of Hope's shows in January 1968 when he was recuperating at a MASH unit just prior to the Tet offensive: "I'd heard that Hope was coming, so I walked out of the hospital, asking people along the way for directions." Hegi came over a hill to a site that had been an empty field the day before to find a throng of thousands, all helicoptered in for the show, before a stage and a massive PA system. Hegi said that Hope's favorite tactic for getting laughs was to make jokes about other branches of the service. "He'd put on a beret to make fun of the Green Berets," Hegi said in a 1998 interview. "Then he'd put on a sailor's cap to make fun of the navy." Hegi, who now owns a golfing range, noticed from his vantage

❝ Don't **worry** about **those riots** you've heard about **back in the States.** They'll send you to **survival school** before you go back there. **❞** —*Bob Hope in Vietnam*

Left: **Bob Hope receives a medal from President John F. Kennedy for service to the armed forces. Hope quipped that the bronze medallion, "wouldn't be quite so heavy if I'd have gotten that nose job."** Opposite: **Bob Hope entertains soldiers in South Vietnam in 1967. Hope supported the troops in his own inimitable style.**

Right: **Jet-setting Bob arrives with his entourage.** Hope said sarcastically of retirement, **"Now, I'll finally get the opportunity to do what I've always wanted to—travel."** Opposite: **Bob wears a silly hat aboard the USS John F. Kennedy. One of Hope's favorite tricks for entertaining the troops was to wear different hats representing different branches of the service as props for his jokes.**

IN THE SA
WELCOMES
BOB + CO
VF-14
USS JOHN F. KE
UNITED STATES SHIP JOHN
CVA-67
CVA 67

Above: **President Nixon honors Bob Hope with an honorary college degree from Georgetown University in 1969.** Opposite: **Hope's support of the United States' involment in Vietnam, in particular of the soldiers who fought in the war, earned him some enemies back home. Hope toured college campuses in an attempt to woo young people back to his side, but the country was already too deeply divided. Hope's loyalties seemed to go beyond the thorny politics of the time to reach out for the war-weary soldiers who always appreciated his shows.**

point among the crowd of twelve thousand that Hope also changed his golf club throughout his routine. "He knew how to work the crowd," Hegi said. "The men down front got riled up when he'd chase the women, and of course there was the one lucky soldier who got to go onstage and have a dance." At the time Hope was touring with Ann-Margaret, who led the audience in singing Christmas songs. The response was typical of most of Hope's shows. "There's such a thing as comic relief," Hegi said. "In a situation where you aren't sleeping, listening for every noise, it's just nice to relax for a few hours and laugh. You don't do a lot of laughing in the jungle."

After the Tet offensive, Hope's attitude toward his mission in Vietnam began to change as the war became less popular and there were more student protests back home. In 1969 Hope went on a tour of college campuses to address the issue of supporting the war. He performed his act as usual, but closed with a serious plea to support U.S. soldiers in Vietnam. Hope continued to keep friends inside the White House. When he invited President Richard Nixon to attend his daughter Linda's wedding, Nixon sent Spiro Agnew in his stead, and Hope and Agnew became friends. Even though Hope claimed his politics were neutral, his friendship with Agnew and his support of the increasingly unpopular war in Vietnam inextricably linked him with the right wing of American politics. In his memoir *Five Women I Love: Bob Hope's Vietnam Story,* he wrote, "I might as well admit it. I have no politics where the boys are concerned....And if backing these kids to the hilt means offending a few part-time citizens and losing a few points in the Nielsens, then so be it." In related statements, Hope even went so far as to suggest that, while their peers were risking their lives for their country, the protesters gave aid and comfort to the enemy.

The North Vietnamese considered Hope a target, and he missed having one of his public appearances bombed by ten minutes because of a faulty timing device. Security was stepped up and eventually all the members of the company were armed, even onstage. Despite these precautions, there was no real difference between the shows in 1943 and in Vietnam. His act was still a variety show, updated with more contemporary stars, but the purpose was the same. Hope visited hospitals and provided a few hours of distraction for the men in the field. In 1972, Hope played what he called his last Christmas show in Vietnam. Still, he managed to continue to entertain troops at bases around the States during the holidays every year.

SOLDIERING ON

Certainly Hope was not immune to the aging process, but when he was dancing and chasing girls onstage, he always appeared as if he were. He had experienced eye trouble all throughout the 1950s and 1960s. Now his eyesight began to fail, and he underwent several major surgeries, facing a real possibility of blindness, beginning in early 1970. He was ordered to rest or risk losing his sight. Though he slowed down a bit, he went back on tour in 1983, visiting U.S. troops in Beirut, Lebanon. In 1987 he did a world tour for U.S. military personnel in the Atlantic, the Pacific, and the Persian Gulf. Before the start of the Gulf War, he began entertaining troops during the buildup, and by Christmas of that year (1990) he was playing to soldiers in Saudi Arabia for Operation Desert Shield.

Above: **Hope donned traditional Arab headgear before embarking on a trip to Lebanon in 1983 to entertain the troops at Christmas.**
Opposite: **By the time Hope did his final tour of duty, before the U.S. troops in Saudi Arabia, the singers had changed from the big band era-type to R & B stars the Pointer Sisters, but the formula—gags, girls, and golf—was essentially the same. And so were the big laughs from appreciative GI audiences.**

BOB HOPE IN PROFILE

Above: **Hope's star on the Hollywood walk of fame lies right next to that of his wife, Dolores.** Opposite: **Hope wisecracks about his oversized portrait, which was the backdrop for his 1986 TV special "Happy Birthday Bob—50 Stars Salute Your 50 Years with NBC," starring, among others, Elizabeth Taylor and Alf.**

After World War II there were enormous adjustments to be made, both by the United States and Bob Hope. One of his first peacetime ambitions was to form his own independent production company, and after haggling with Paramount for years over the terms, he was finally allowed to form Hope Enterprises, Inc., in 1945. Twelve years later it financed its first film, *Paris Holiday.* The company still exists today, doing brisk business selling Hope's videos via the Internet.

After the war, Bob and Dolores decided to adopt another baby. In October 1946, when they went to pick up a four-month-old baby girl named Nora from the adoption agency, they were surprised and delighted to find that there was also a baby boy for them. The boy, Kelly, completed the Hope family. With the postwar additions to his family, Hope stayed closer to home than he had for years. He went back to Hollywood full-time, making some of his best movies, including *My Favorite Brunette, Road to Rio, Paleface,* and *Sorrowful Jones* (1949).

Without the troops' heightened laughter and topical army jokes, Hope found it increasingly difficult to keep his *Pepsodent Radio Hour* fresh and exciting. Reviewers became critical, yet the show's formula was still successful in that Hope's ratings remained high, at least in part because of the broadcasts from military bases that he continued during peacetime. Hope hired Doris Day as a singer, and America's favorite goody-two-shoes proved to be not only a lovely singer but also an adept comedienne. She described the atmosphere on the show in her autobiography: "Bob used to call me Jut-Butt and say, 'Hey, J.B., we could play a nice game of bridge on your ass.'" Hope referred to her as J.B. on the air, but only the cast understood the joke. Day said that Hope's teasing helped ease the tension and helped her forget about her stage fright, which nearly paralyzed her before each performance: "My overwhelming memory of that show was being stuck in the bathroom with the butterflies." Like all members of the *Pepsodent Radio Hour* cast, Day was expected to participate in the on-air skits and between-segment comic exchanges that were part of the show's successful formula.

Hope reads his monologue in the talking-heads world of early television. This was Hope's first TV broadcast, filmed live on Easter Sunday, 1950.

Not quite the Partridge Family. Always eager to work his relatives into show business, Bob had this family photo taken with Linda on harp, Tony on the tuba, Kelly and Nora each on guitar, and Dolores at the piano.

STAR OF STAGE, SCREEN, AND TV!

In the late 1940s, radio began to feel television take a bite from its audience. Milton Berle's show became a hit despite the fact that most Americans didn't own TV sets. People often gathered at the house of a friend who had a set, making watching the tiny flickering screen a social event. Hope made regular appearances on television during this time, with regular guest spots on Bing Crosby's *Kraft Show*. He frequently used these opportunities to promote the movies he made with Bing. Hope realized that any exposure in the media would be bound to help his radio show, but he was skeptical about doing a show of his own on television. He felt that the medium was a novelty that might not prove worth the trouble of giving up a proven radio show, and when NBC offered him his own weekly television program, he declined.

Fate stepped in and put Bob Hope on TV. In 1950, he was in a car accident on his way to Paramount Studios to film retakes for *Fancy Pants*. His injuries were enough to put his leg in a cast. He couldn't complete the picture with a cast, but he felt fine otherwise. The workaholic Hope decided he could still play before the talking-heads medium of television and took NBC up on the offer to let him host a variety show. He did what he thought would be a onetime comedy variety hour, broadcast on Easter Sunday in 1950. The show was a smash

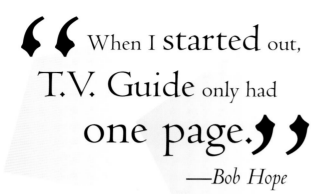

When I started out, T.V. Guide only had one page.

—*Bob Hope*

hit and the comic variety *Bob Hope Special* was born. Hope was signed by NBC to do six more specials at that time. In 1996, he celebrated his sixtieth year with NBC, which included his radio work for the network, and performed his three hundredth, and last, special, "Bob Hope Laughs with the Presidents."

Hope's first TV show was filmed at the Paramount Theater in New York. While in the Big Apple, Bob was introduced to the cause of cerebral palsy. He was taken to P.S. 135 to meet some children afflicted with the disease, and after the Easter Sunday show, he did a series of fund-raising benefits on his way back across the country to California. Over the years, Hope continued to raise money to battle the disease, and it became one of his favorite charities, a cause for which he played benefit shows and celebrity golf tournaments.

Although his early TV specials were not that different from his radio shows, Hope soon realized the potential of video and that the kind of physical visual comedy he used in his movies could supplement the verbal gags. The variety show was no longer limited to singing, and Hope could use dance acts like the ones on his tours for the troops.

Because of Hope's international stardom and service to the Allied forces, Bob and Dolores Hope meet Queen Elizabeth II in 1947.

PRIVATE PARTS

In 1951 Hope went on a tour of England to benefit war-recovery charities. One of the impoverished English children who came onstage at the end of his show in London was a young Michael Caine. (Years later, the then-famous actor met the comedian again and told him that he was one of the shy urchins who had accepted the check from Hope all those years before.) Hope brought his television costar Marilyn Maxwell with him to England as part of the

Above: **Bob Hope and Marilyn Maxwell sing on Hope's TV show in 1954. Although his long career has been free of the usual Hollywood scandals, Hope was linked romantically with Maxwell in a tell-all story in a tabloid called *Hollywood Confidential*.**

company, and the pair were romantically linked when they took a weekend vacation together in Ireland at the end of the tour. They were spotted walking arm in arm down the fairway while they were playing golf. The press did not report the vacation as a lover's tryst until a Hollywood starlet named Barbara Peyton, who'd worked on Hope's TV show, sold her story to *Hollywood Confidential Magazine* in 1954. Peyton insinuated that she'd had an affair with Hope and that it ended because he took up with Maxwell. Whether or not there was any truth to Peyton's story, Bob's wife, Dolores, didn't seem worried. Of the *Confidential* article she said, "Every woman's husband is attractive to some other woman. I have tried to do the only thing a woman can do—keep busy, try to remain interesting, and cling to my own conceits. When doubt has troubled me, I think, 'But why shouldn't he love me before anyone else?'"

As the Hope clan grew, Bob was making shrewd investments to provide for their future. In the mid-1950s he was one of the highest-paid performers in Hollywood, picking up paychecks for both his film and television work. But Hope's real wealth was derived from real estate. When he first came to Hollywood, he and Bing Crosby had purchased thousands of acres in the San Fernando valley. *Road* costar Anthony Quinn said that Hope and Crosby could often be seen wheeling and dealing on the set. "They were carving up the valley," he said, "deciding who would get what between takes." By the mid-1970s the value of Hope's land holdings had appreciated so greatly that he was estimated to be worth $400 million. Of

What's Black and White and Seen All Over?

In November 1950 Hope did a TV show for NBC with Frigidaire as his sponsor. He was playing before an air force audience in Korea during an escalation in the conflict. The show costarred Marilyn Maxwell, Les Brown and His Orchestra, the Three Taylor Maids, and an African-American tap-dance act called the High-Hatters. Their novelty dance routine was similar to the type of dancing Bob had done when he had started out, so he naturally joined them onstage at the end of the show, linking arms vaudeville-style for the finale. His appearance at the end of the act, a surprise to the audience, was a showstopper.

This was Hope's quiet way of integrating his television show. He seemed disinterested in the civil rights movement in the 1960s when he was questioned about it, and those interviews only served to distance himself from the youth culture of the time. But in 1950 he had danced with two black men on national television, ten years before Frank Sinatra was considered a pioneer for integrating his nightclub act by allowing Sammy Davis, Jr., into his Rat Pack. The High-Hatters were booked for the Korean tour because they were popular with black soldiers. To Hope it was about show business, and if he had any idea that what he was doing was out of the ordinary, he never let on.

course, Hope complained that he was poor from paying property taxes on all that land, and he continued to keep as tight a schedule as his health would allow.

Like Frank Sinatra, Hope was one of the most powerful men in show business. Unlike Sinatra, Hope had an almost pristine image, despite the *Confidential* story. When two Hollywood con men decided to kidnap Frank Sinatra, Jr., they did so only after passing

Hope is famous for his love of golf and is often credited with popularizing the sport in the United States. He's got a putting green in his backyard, so he's never far from the action. Since World War II, he's appeared on stage with a putter as a prop.

Bob Hope poses in 1996 for a publicity shot for his final TV special, "Bob Hope Laughs with the Presidents."
Former President George Bush, President Bill Clinton, and former President Gerald Ford were cheered by a
gallery full of secret servicemen.

up the opportunity to kidnap Tony Hope because of all the work his father had done for the troops. Even cynical criminals loved Bob Hope.

POLITICS AND THE PUTTING GREEN

Hope's friendships within the White House brought him political power. In the two films in which Hope portrayed politicians, *Louisiana Purchase* and *Beau James* (1957), his characters commented on the similarities between show business and politics. He frequently joked about Ronald Reagan's position as governor of California and then as president, but Hope admired Reagan's ability to be taken seriously as a politician while still maintaining an affable public persona. Hope's visibility as an entertainer who understood politics enough to joke about it convinced a group of California businessmen in 1965 that Bob Hope should run for president. Hope was sorry to tell them that since he was born in England, he wasn't eligible. He joked, "Besides, I'd have to move to a smaller house." He'd just had a putting green put in his backyard at his Toluca Lake home.

Even Hope's favorite pastime, golf, became part of his work routine. He began playing celebrity golf tournaments in the early 1940s. By 1964, Palm Springs had renamed its Palm Springs Classic the Bob Hope Desert Classic. Hope was in charge of the event, lining up some of the greatest professional golfers, from Jack Nicklaus to Arnold Palmer, and plenty of celebrity amateurs, including Crosby and Sinatra. He transformed the tournament from a small local fund raiser to the largest charity golf tournament in the country. He got Chrysler to sponsor it, and the tournament was shown on television every year, giving Hope even more

Above: **The Hope family in 1968. From left to right: Tony, Dolores, Bob, Linda, Nora, and Kelly.** Opposite, top: **Tina Louise, Hope, Jane Wyman, and Leslie Nielsen were part of the cast in the disastrous counterculture spoof *How to Commit Marriage.*** Opposite, bottom: **Hope does a pratfall for his final film, *Cancel My Reservation,* about a talk-show host who goes on vacation and becomes embroiled in a murder mystery.**

exposure in the medium. Today Hope is credited with popularizing the sport in the United States, if only to give the average person a base of knowledge to understand his golf anecdotes. He paraded before thousands of GIs swinging a club and wearing plaid trousers as if he were just playing through a rough spot on the course. He golfed with presidents from Eisenhower to Clinton. And when a rumor circulated on the Internet in 1998 that Bob Hope had died at age ninety-five, Hope said, "The news of my passing is untrue. You got me off the golf course to call this in."

CANCEL THIS MOVIE

Hope's film career faced difficulty in the late 1960s and early 1970s. Comedy, like all of American culture, was being transformed by rebellion. One man, Lenny Bruce, picked up a microphone and used comedy as a form of protest. Hope's brand of comedy was anything but rebellious; Hope was about escapism, not confrontation. Still, he appreciated Lenny Bruce and other young comedians, and in a 1973 interview with *Playboy* magazine Hope said, "Mort Sahl and Woody Allen—those guys are great. But my favorite was Lenny Bruce. . . . He had so much greasepaint in his blood it came out in his act. That's what I loved. He talked our language." This was the language of comedians and entertainers—just as Bob Hope had spoken the language of soldiers in World War II.

Hope's ability to speak anyone's language was in doubt when he made *How to Commit Marriage* (1969), his version of *I Love You Alice B. Toklas,* which featured James Gleason and Tina Louise mocking the hippie generation. The film did not fare well at the box office, partly because the script wasn't too sharp and partly because Hope's skirt-chasing persona

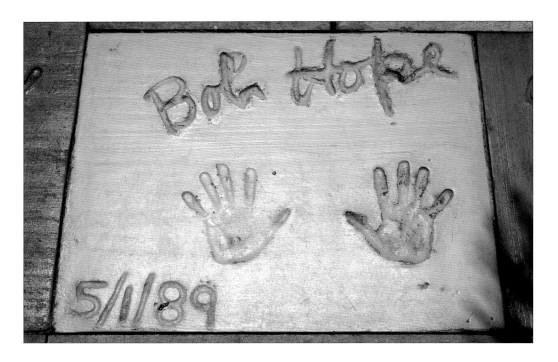

was becoming unseemly for a man in his late sixties. The movie that nearly did in his production company, his film career, and most of the cast and crew was *Cancel My Reservation* (1972). The script was written by Arthur Marx, Groucho's son, and other proven Hope gag writers. They came up with a screenplay, based on a Louis L'Amour novel, for a comedic thriller set in Arizona on an Indian reservation.

The idea was intriguing in theory, combining the most successful elements of Hope's detective comedies, such as *My Favorite Blonde* (1942), and the clichés of the Wild West he had parodied in the *Paleface* movies. The plot surrounds an overworked Los Angeles talk-show host (Hope) who is having marital trouble. He goes on a vacation to Arizona and gets accused of murdering a young Indian woman. Ralph Bellamy plays the bad guy, a landowner who has Hope framed for the murder. Hope's wife, played by Eva Marie Saint, arrives and helps her husband solve the crime and exonerate himself. The studio was pleased to have Hope and Saint as a screen couple since they were close enough in age to pull it off and had had good chemistry in *That Certain Feeling* (1956).

However, problems plagued production from the start, and Hope was never satisfied with the script. Marx described the atmosphere on the set as near revolt when shooting went over schedule and the cast and crew were forced to stay in non-air-conditioned trailers in the desert. Hope demanded constant changes in the script because he felt it wasn't funny enough. He constantly injected new jokes into the scenes. Director Paul Bogart wasn't prepared for this, nor was he as acquiescent as the directors of the *Road* movies had been about Hope's ad-libbing. Bogart tried to pull out of the picture but was told that the studio wouldn't allow it.

Above: **Bob Hope and George Burns celebrate Burns' 95th birthday with a vaudeville dance number. As a kid on the vaudeville circuit, Hope watched star George Burns from the wings.** Left: **Hope and Burns are dressed in traditional vaudeville garb for a skit on the TV special "The Burns and Hope Show."**

Since the story had a serious mystery to solve, Bogart thought all the silly jokes just didn't work. Hope added an almost unrelated dream sequence at the end in which Bing Crosby makes a cameo, which didn't do much to help a movie that was already bordering on incoherent. When the film was released, it premiered at Radio City Music Hall, the first Hope film to do so.

Unfortunately, the movie was not well received; not only was the plot disjointed but the humor seemed completely out of touch with the times. In one scene, Hope is supposed to meet with the Indian leader, played by Native American actor Dan George. George insisted that he not lose his dignity and that there be no racist jokes in the script. He was shown one of the many drafts, but after his scene was filmed, Hope had his writers make up Indian jokes in poor taste and put them in the subtitles of what George was saying. Pauline Kael called the movie "a new low in filmmaking." *Cancel My Reservation* was Hope's last major role in a feature film. He managed to make audiences forget it, making cameos in *The Muppet Movie* and *Spies Like Us.*

HOPE SPRINGS ETERNAL

Hope's support of the Vietnam War may have distanced him from the youth culture of the 1960s, but it did little to harm his TV ratings. His yearly specials continued to be among the highest-rated programs on television. Hope updated his Honey Chile routine from radio, dropping the southern accent and using whatever spokesmodel was at hand as his

stooge. Brooke Shields became a favorite and appeared repeatedly throughout the late 1970s and 1980s. Although Shields never took off as a dramatic actress, she learned comic timing and a self-deprecating sense of humor from Hope, which she went on to use in her own sitcom, *Suddenly Susan*—an example of Hope's influence in virtually every mass medium.

Hope's status as a comedic statesman took him to China in 1979. While Nixon's 1972 visit had heralded the era of détente and opened China for diplomatic relations, Hope's visit proved that comedy wasn't always an effective tool for diplomacy. Comedian Dave Thomas, of The Second City comedy troupe in Toronto, lampooned the visit by impersonating Hope and imagining all the trouble that his writers would have finding jokes to appeal to a Chinese audience. Hope saw the sketch when he and Thomas worked together on his 1992 TV special, "Bob Hope Salutes Young Comedians." Hope said, "What you don't know is, that was exactly what it was like for us. I had to do my monologue with an interpreter."

Bob Hope slowed down considerably in his later years, spending time with his four grandchildren, but he was never able to stop working completely. When asked why he did not just retire and go fishing, he said, "Fish don't laugh." He obviously thrived on laughter. It kept him going through four shows a day in four wars. He holds Guinness world records for having been the most decorated American civilian of all time and for having entertained the most people of any performer in history. In 1998, he was knighted by both the Pope and the Queen of England, only two of many honors that continue to pour in for the entertainer.

Above: **After more than sixty years, Bob and Dolores Hope were still each other's main costars in life.** Opposite: **Hope poses with the same type of radio microphone he used in the early days of his career. After sixty years with NBC, he became a free agent in 1997.**

Most Honored Entertainer

Hope holds two entries in the *Guinness Book of World Records*: the first as most honored entertainer and the second for the longest contract with a single network. The second record was set in 1996 as he celebrated his sixtieth year with NBC, first as a radio star, then as host of numerous TV specials. His trophy room includes such trinkets as honorary Oscars, Knighthoods from the Queen of England and the Pope, forty-nine honorary degrees, and more than seven hundred awards for his contributions to charities.

Left: **Hope plants a kiss on the bust of himself at the dedication of the Bob Hope USO building in Washington, D.C., in 1985.** Opposite, top: **Bob Hope cuts up with President Ronald Reagan at the taping of Hope's TV special "Aerial Rodeo and Bob Hope Gala Spectacular" in 1987. Reagan's background as an actor and well-known abilities as a storyteller made their on-air banter especially lively.** Opposite, bottom: **Bob Hope stands next to the street sign that bears his name, near the entrance to NBC Studios in Burbank, California.**

ON THE MOUNT RUSHMORE OF COMEDY

In a 1998 article in *The New York Times,* late-night talk-show host Conan O'Brien said that Bob Hope, for all his influence on comedy, was lost on comics of O'Brien's generation: "To most of my friends, Bob Hope is the guy in a blazer who's doing a monologue off cue cards or who's dressed as a Cabbage Patch Doll doing a sketch with Brooke Shields." But looking back on Hope's earlier work in radio and in film during the 1940s and 1950s, one sees the fresh, ad-libbed style of comedy riddled with inside jokes that hip, younger comedians like O'Brien are doing today. Conan continued: "There are things I do every night on the show, [like] growl at beautiful women, that come from Bob Hope."

Bob Hope was so successful that he became an institution, almost forgotten because of his venerability. O'Brien said that Hope is one of the faces on the Mount Rushmore of comedy. His persona, especially in the *Road* movies, became part of our cultural memory, part of our lexicon. Bob Hope is such an integral element of our comedic language that it is easy to forget that the persona he created had no forerunner. Ty Burr, critic for *Entertainment Weekly,* said in a 1997 interview, "Bob Hope was the first neurotic comedian."

Hope's wisecracking, cowardly character, forever in comic pursuit of a beautiful lady only to lose her in the final scene, has been borrowed by comic actors from Jerry Lewis to Woody Allen. Allen's film *Love and Death* is an upscale version of the type of genre parody Hope mastered in the 1940s and 1950s. Allen simply injects his cowardly Casanova wanna-be into a *War and Peace*–type story line. The subject matter is more intellectual, but the basic humor is pure Hope.

Opposite: Hope delivers a monologue for television in 1984. Above: **Hope's dancing and singing were integral to his comic persona, as was his sometimes unusual clothing.**

Left: **Bob Hope poses on the golf course in the 1940s. Hope started playing golf in the spring of 1930, when fellow Broadway performers The Diamond Brothers invited him along for an afternoon. Ten years later he was playing an average of 72 holes per week.**

The adult cartoon character Duckman, a Daffy Duck for the 1990s with the voice of Jason Alexander, once devoted an entire episode to a parody of Hope and Crosby called "Road to Dendron." Duckman carries out such *Road* standards as the pattycake punch and sly musical numbers. When the heroine takes a decided liking to Duckman, his sidekick, Orson, says, "You realize this means we can no longer have a friendly, song-filled rivalry for her."

When one starts to take notice, it quickly becomes clear that Bob Hope is everywhere in popular culture. He was always keenly aware of his public image, and his staff of PR people, whom he employed since the late 1930s, never passed up an opportunity to get his name in the papers. Yet Hope was a private man who kept his emotions close to home. In his many memoirs he freely related anecdotes from his public life, but talked little about his wife, four children, and four grandchildren except to make a joke at his own expense. On his seventy-fifth birthday, after listening for hours to tributes from family, colleagues, and political big shots, Hope said, "I think I'm about seventy-five. I don't know, I've lied to so many different women. Dolores—that's a joke."

Filmography

Going Spanish. Educational Films, 1934.
Paree, Paree. Warner Bros., 1934.
Bob's Busy Day. Educational Films, 1934.
Watch the Birdie. Educational Films, 1935.
Soup for Nuts. Educational Films, 1935.
The Old Grey Mayor. Warner Bros., 1935.
Double Exposure. Warner Bros., 1935.
Shop Talk. Warner Bros., 1936.
Calling All Tars. Warner Bros., 1936.
The Big Broadcast of 1938. Paramount, 1938.
Thanks for the Memory. Paramount, 1938.
Give Me a Sailor. Paramount, 1938.
College Swing. Paramount, 1938.
Some Like It Hot. Paramount, 1939.
Never Say Die. Paramount, 1939.
The Cat and the Canary. Paramount, 1939.
The Ghost Breakers. Paramount, 1940.
Road to Singapore. Paramount, 1940.
Road to Zanzibar. Paramount, 1941.
Nothing But the Truth. Paramount, 1941.
Caught in the Draft. Paramount, 1941.
Louisiana Purchase. Paramount, 1941.
Star Spangled Rhythm. Paramount, 1942.
Road to Morocco. Paramount, 1942.
My Favorite Blonde. Paramount, 1942.
Hedda Hopper's Hollywood No. 4. Paramount, 1942.
Show Business at War. Paramount, 1943.
Let's Face It. Paramount, 1943.
Combat America. Paramount, 1943.
They Got Me Covered. Goldwyn-RKO, 1943.
The Princess and the Pirate. Goldwyn-RKO, 1944.
Road to Utopia. Paramount, 1945.
Monsieur Beaucaire. Paramount, 1946.
Where There's Life. Paramount, 1947.
Road to Rio. Paramount, 1947.
My Favorite Brunette. Paramount, 1947.

Variety Girl. Paramount, 1947.
Paleface. Paramount, 1948.
Sorrowful Jones. Paramount, 1949.
The Great Lover. Paramount, 1949.
Fancy Pants. Paramount, 1950.
The Lemon Drop Kid. Paramount, 1951.
Son of Paleface. Paramount, 1952.
Road to Bali. Paramount, 1952.
The Greatest Show on Earth. 1952.
Off Limits. Paramount, 1953.
Here Come the Girls. Paramount, 1953.
Casanova's Big Night. Paramount, 1954.
The Seven Little Foys. Paramount, 1955.
That Certain Feeling. Paramount, 1956.
The Iron Petticoat. MGM, 1956.
Beau James. Paramount, 1957.
Paris Holiday. United Artists, 1958.
Five Pennies. United Artists, 1959.
Alias Jesse James. United Artists, 1959.
Facts of Life. United Artists, 1960.
Bachelor in Paradise. MGM, 1961.
Road to Hong Kong. United Artists, 1962.
Critic's Choice. Warner Bros., 1963.
Call Me Bwana. United Artists, 1963.
Global Affair. MGM, 1964.
I'll Take Sweden. United Artists, 1965.
Not with My Wife, You Don't. United Artists, 1966.
Boy, Did I Get a Wrong Number! United Artists, 1966.
Eight on the Lam. United Artists, 1967.
The Private Navy of Sgt. O'Farrell. United Artists, 1968.
How to Commit Marriage. Cinerama, 1969.
Cancel My Reservation. Warner Bros., 1972.
The Muppet Movie. Sir Lew Grade, 1979.
Spies Like Us. Warner Bros., 1985.A

Bibliography

Faith, William Robert. Bob Hope: A Life in Comedy. New York: Doubleday, 1982.

Hope, Bob, Five Women I Love: Bob Hope's Vietnam Story. New York: Doubleday, 1966.

————. I Never Left Home. New York: Home Guide Publications, 1943.

————. The Road to Hollywood. New York: Doubleday, 1977.

Marx, Arthur. The Secret Life of Bob Hope. Emeryville, Calif.: Publishers Group West, 1993.

O'Brien, Conan. "A Bob Hope Clause Means Without Him, All Bets Are Off." The New York Times, 24 May 1998.

Thomas, Dave. SCTV: Behind the Scenes. Toronto: M & S Publishing, 1996.